AF702759

get out there
and do something
about injustice

get out there and do something about injustice

by Margaret E. Kuhn

Friendship Press · New York

Library of Congress Catalogue Card Number: 77–182979

Printed in the United States of America

contents

foreword

Margaret Kuhn has given us a different sort of book.

First, it's a book about doingfaithandhavingjustice. That's right, all one thing. In the more usual combinations we talk of "having faith" and "doing something for the cause of justice," splitting the world of experience into the half-truths of "private realm" and "public affairs," of "spiritual life" and "social action."

The times demand a new integrity. Justice, like faith, is for having; faith, like justice, is for doing. When justice becomes a present possession and faith is a way of doing our living, we'll all be a giant step closer to the dreams of our hearts, the Utopias of the mind, the Kingdom of our God.

A second characteristic of the book results from the first. As faith is not just for contemplation, these pages are not here merely to be read. They represent ideas to struggle with, signs to follow, stimuli to a more human, useful life. This is an action handbook.

To all of you who live where faith and justice must come together, we commend it.

Ward L. Kaiser
Senior Editor
Friendship Press

introduction

This handbook has been written to respond to a new age, a new situation in the churches, and a new situation in the world where human beings live, work and develop a common life.

It is intended to be a guide for reflection, group inquiry and action. Hopefully it will be useful to adults and young people in the Christian community in responding to what God is doing in the world.

The purpose of the reflection, inquiry, action approach is threefold:

1. To demonstrate how theological reflection and social analysis guide and empower us in what we think and do in this new age.
2. To suggest specific ways in which Christians as persons and groups can proclaim "the good news."

3. To affirm in specific human situations and social issues God's continuing action in the world.

Many church members are concerned about the decline in church membership, church influence and church support. Those who are troubled about growing dissent within congregations make strenuous efforts to keep the church "safe" by glossing over controversy and opposing involvement in social and political matters. Many of us are afraid of dissent, quite unaware that controversy can be creative and redemptive.

The assumption is widely held that the churches are being torn apart by the social activists. Jazz in the chancel, demonstrations in the streets, ministries in crash pads and coffee houses have seemed to be disturbing departures from the familiar tried-and-true ways of proclaiming the gospel. There is much talk about the need to build bridges to bring people together, yet sometimes reaching alienated young people and hostile minorities may not be accomplished by going over bridges, but by leaping into troubled waters and deep canyons, where rage and despair abound. Resources for survival in such leaps of faith are briefly described in these chapters.

Awareness of the activity of God implies that:

1. God is the living God.
2. God is actively working out his purpose for mankind through every age and through every situation.
3. We must use all our human resources to ascertain the reality of the situation, that is, its truths.
4. We have the gift of Holy Spirit to lead us to the truth.
5. When we discern what God is doing, we are called to cooperate with him.
6. God accepts us as we are, with our limitations and powers, and will not call us to do what is beyond us.[1]

This handbook contains suggestions of material to be used in a variety of ways by a variety of groups of young people and adults. As a traditional "course" for study groups it could be divided into at least ten sessions, two for each of the five chapters. As a stimulus for action and theological reflection the starting point might be some first-hand research through careful investigation of what is happening in "our town."

Some groups will move away from the

---

[1] Adapted from, *Christian Social Ethics in a Changing World,* ed., John C. Bennett. (New York: Association Press, 1966).

"traditional" and experiment with new uses of the contents, for example, as:

- A tool for community analysis, leading to some new approaches to a community problem.
- An aid to church officers as they plan and evaluate mission and ministry.
- Subject matter for a series of Faith and Justice vocational seminars of teachers, nurses, building contractors, realtors, lawyers, probing the problems of professional groups in theological-ethical terms.
- Questions for lively and live radio and/or TV panels.
- A teach-in at a nearby college or university.
- A launching pad for institutional review and reform in church-related institutions.
- Action-research to determine the priorities for mission, a profile of church membership within a diocese, presbytery or metropolitan council of churches.
- Roman Catholic-Protestant dialogue about church renewal.
- Many more inventive ideas dreamed up by the group.

This handbook does not however stand alone; further help on this study will be found in other resources, including *Grace at Point Zero* by Loren E. Halvorson, and *Guide on "Faith and Justice" for Adult and Youth Groups* by L. Wayne Bryan, both published by Friendship Press.

Probably the most creative use will be made by persons brought together by common concern for an issue. Input from community groups and students from colleges in the area is extremely valuable to broaden understanding and increase possibilities for continued interaction of church and community forces. Hopefully high school and college students will be participants in research and fact finding that will require action. Ralph Nader's young raiders have shown what perceptive young people can do to expose injustice and exploitation.

Groups already working on such issues as the "Crusade against Hunger," prison reform, or the rehabilitation of drug addicts will find some new approaches in Chapters 4 and 5. The book supplements background materials already available from denominational and ecumenical sources. Each section is open-ended and wide open to innovation by local leaders and groups.

Each chapter has material for theological reflection and specific options for social involvement and action. Each chapter will suggest group processes to increase awareness and involvement. Conveners of the action groups are assumed to be enablers, not dictators or people with all the answers. Leadership is a dynamic force shifting from person to person, depending on the issue to be tackled and the problem to be resolved. We have consciously avoided using the term "leader" since leadership *flows through* every human group, and is not confined to one or two "heads" who may be elected or even self-appointed.

These elements will be important:

1. The openness of group members to each other, and to new, untested ideas, willingness to listen to different and conflicting points of view, and tolerance, if not acceptance of new concepts.
2. The convener's ability to coordinate and stimulate response, assisting the group to move toward their stated goals.
3. The free and responsible participation of each group member.
4. The opportunity for the group to develop its own ideas and options for study and action, using the text as a launching pad.

In this new age a lot is happening in group process and group theory—the emphasis on body contact, body language, feelings, emotional vs. cerebral response, encounter groups and the complex training programs in systems planning and analysis. A few group approaches are suggested in the various chapters. More should be explored and tried out.

Two new and perceptive methods to change the class oppression found in women's groups originated in the Women's Liberation Movement—the Lot System and the Disc System. The women had observed that those with better educations (made possible by their class and economic backgrounds) dominated the meetings, wrote all the papers, edited the news sheets and manipulated and intimidated the sisters who had less education. Robin Morgan, editor of *Sisterhood is Powerful,* describes the systems. The Lot System consists of two sets of lots, one for *creative tasks* like writing papers, attending conferences, dealing with the media, and the other for *work tasks* like answering mail, mimeographing literature, and so on. Each person draws for each task, so that no person gets stereotyped. The Disc System is an ingenious way to keep some women from monopolizing meetings, while others never utter a word. Each member begins the meeting with a certain number of discs. Every time she speaks, beyond a simple "yes" or "no," she must spend one disc. It is said that in the first meeting where the Disc System was tried, nobody had any discs after the first fifteen minutes. At the second meeting silence reigned as the sisters hoarded their discs. Gradually the system worked its way into the consciousness of the members as a "symbol for the need to listen to each other without monopolizing or interrupting. The system also encouraged the women to speak up."

Much more conscious thought must be given to developing and experimenting with new structures that free people to think and interact creatively. Bureaucracies built on hierarchial systems have been found highly resistant to change. More flexible arrangements must emerge, and the churches should be in the vanguard of such experimentation.

The use of this handbook should offer an opportunity to examine fundamentals in our Christian faith so that we may meet the future with some assurance and joy.

chapter

·1·

SIGNS OF THESE TIMES

Ours is the age of self-determination and liberation—liberation from oppression and paternalism, liberation from hunger and want, liberation from fear. Signs of change and newness are all around us. Christians in every age have been called to read the signs of the times, and there are awesome signs in this age for us to read and ponder. Changes have been sweeping through every age of history and prehistory, but their increasing intensity and speed have introduced entirely new elements in our day, for example:

- The cultural revolution which is bringing in new goals and values, changes in life-styles, changes in the family and woman's liberation in society and in the churches.

- The world-wide rebellion and protest of youth.
- The world-wide liberation movements among the oppressed peoples of Southern Africa, Southeast Asia and South America.
- The affirmation of our modern society as a pluralistic society—not a melting pot.
- The growth of grass roots organizations to enable the powerless and poor to determine their own destiny.
- The impact of computers and systems analysis on vocations, production of goods and services, decision-making and the development of societal policies.

In this age of change and revolution there is great urgency to discover our roots and origins—what abides in the midst of change. At the same time we must see and grasp the new opportunities for faithfulness that God has put before us.

"Faith and Justice," two elements we focus on in this action handbook, are joined in our human situation in the strivings of men and women to be truly human and free and to find community with others.

Tabloids, books and scholarly journals report many of the signs of the times; but even more telling may be our own encounter with change and how we regard this new age. Because many of the issues and problems are complex, not easily understood or tackled without great social concern, the tendency of many of us is to turn away from the signs and pursue our own private interests. We are often numbed by crises, convinced that things are beyond our control or influence. There are great differences of opinion about such matters as welfare, poverty and racial justice. Most of us settle for what our favorite columnist writes, without doing our own thinking.

The statements quoted here from current writers and social analysts show some of the signs of our times and different reactions to them:

In the three short decades between now and the 21st century millions of ordinary, psychologically normal people will face an abrupt collision with the future. Citizens of the world's richest and most technologically advanced nations, many of them will find it increasingly painful to keep up with the incessant demand for change that characterizes our time. For them, the future will have arrived too soon. . . .

Western society for the past 300 years has been caught up in a fire storm of change. This storm, far from abating, now appears to be gathering force and unprecedented impact. It spawns in its wake all sorts of curious social flora—from psychedelic churches and "free universities" to science cities in the arctic and wife-swap clubs in California . . . There are married priests and atheist ministers and Jewish Zen Buddhists. We have pop . . . and op . . . Playboy clubs and homosexual movie theatres . . . amphetamines and tranquilizers . . . anger, affluence, and oblivion.

The culture shock phenomenon accounts for much of the bewilderment, frustration, and disorientation that plagues Americans in their dealings with other societies. It causes a breakdown in communication, a misreading of reality, an inability to cope. Yet culture shock is relatively mild in comparison with the much more serious malady, future shock, the dizzying disorientation brought on by the premature arrival of the future . . . The malaise, mass neurosis, irrationality, and free-floating violence already apparent in contemporary life are merely a foretaste of what may lie ahead unless we come to understand and treat this disease.

Future shock is a time phenomenon, a product of greatly accelerated rate of change in society. It is culture shock in one's own society.

Alvin Toffler, *Future Shock* (New York: Random House, Inc., 1970). Used by permission.

Computers invent work for other computers. Out of many dangerous possibilities which this suggests I take only one: the proposal to create a Master-Memory in which all the information about everyone could be stored and capable of instant retrieval. The arguments are highly plausible. What is wrong in bringing together information which in scattered detail already exists? Today the U.S. Central Intelligence Agency has at least 15,000 agents feeding back "intelligence" which goes into a computer to be personalized, and, therefore, "objective". . . We have "Satellite Diplomacy" which, by instant communication has changed the whole status of the foreigh offices and diplomats of the world.

Lord Ritchie Calder, "Our Problems are Here on Earth," *The Center Magazine,* March/April, 1971.

The Women's Liberation Movement exists where three or four friends or neighbors decide to meet regularly and talk about their personal lives. It also exists in the cells of women's jails, on the welfare lines, in the supermarket, the factory, the convent, the farm, the maternity ward, the street corner, the old ladies' home, the kitchen, the steno pool, the bed. It exists in your mind, and in the political and personal insights that you can contribute to change and shape and help its growth. It is frightening. It is very exhilarating. It is creating history, or rather, *herstory,* and anyway, you cannot escape it.

Robin Morgan, ed., *Sisterhood is Powerful* (New York: Random House, Inc., 1970). Used by permission.

It is very important that we anticipate the issues arising in the genetic control of man. The molecular biologist who has been so successful in unraveling the nature of genetics is now turning his attention to the analysis of the nervous system and brain function at the molecular level. We shall have information in our hands for the control of human behavior far beyond anything we now possess. The process of controlling behavior either by electrode implantation, by drugs, psychological conditioning or some form of brain surgery put very powerful weapons in man's hands . . . .

"The second concern is the matter of other people controlling the behavior of individuals or groups. It is done with cattle in fields by remote control radios. It could be done with people. We know very little about guidelines to help us with such ethical issues. A third issue is the extent to which psychological conditioning really is ethically acceptable. It is being used now with problems like alcoholism and homosexuality. It seems to me to be like the use of the penalties of hell-fire to motivate people away from certain behavior. How much should fear enter into the way we condition people? These are not questions which the church is asking of science, but which science is asking of the world.

> Prof. L. Charles Birch, School of Biological Sciences, University of Sydney, Australia. Opening statement, "Debate on Biology," June 1, 1970, World Council of Churches. Used by permission.

We live in a world which is both shockingly different and radically new in its quality. Accordingly, its problems are not only different but qualitatively new. Such problems cannot be solved along the lines prescribed by our inherited recipes. Recipes are formulas which indicate what is to be done and how. All languages are recipes. Together with all the old prescriptions, traditional theological languages are in crisis because they are unable to handle the ingredients which our present world contains.

The hope is that a new language of faith can be created which may become an effective tool for the transformation of the earth into a place of recovery. Not only that. We hope that the new language can be learned and actually spoken by Christian communities because it is only when this happens that a language becomes powerful enough to inform men's understanding of the world and their activity in it.

The power of words is totally derived from the power of those communities which sustain and utter them. Our task, then, is to create a theological language which can actually be spoken by real communities.

Theology and the Liberation of Man,
A paper by Rubem A. Alves

THEOLOGICAL REFLECTION

Faith and Justice are linked in the theme of his handbook as they are inexorably joined in the life, teachings and death and resurrection of Jesus Christ. Our theme is properly rooted in the Old and New Testaments. The two theological questions: "Who am I?" and "Who are we?" are deep questions of identity and selfhood, as well as indicators of our place in the human community now and in the future.

Faith in the living God and faithfulness to him become real to us only as we reach out to neighbor and brother. Christ himself stated it clearly. How can you love God whom you have not seen when you do not love your neighbor whom you have seen?

Even before his coming into the world as a man-child, the words of Mary's Magnificat made clear that *faith* in God and faithfulness to him impel us to seek mercy and *justice,* in our relationships with others. "He has shown strength with his arm and scattered the proud in the imagination of their hearts. He has put down the mighty from their thrones and exalted those of low degree. He has filled the hungry with good things and the rich he has sent empty away." (Luke 1:51–53)

In *The Secular Congregation* (New York: Harper and Row, Pub., Inc., 1968), Robert A. Raines writes of the Old and New Covenants between God and his people, God's relation to his people and theirs to him and to each other.

The Old Covenant was born out of the sufferings and travail of the Hebrews under Pharoah and the Exodus. Its explicit meaning for the Hebrews who participated in it was liberation from oppression in Egypt, liberation for the future, liberation for life to be lived in freedom as heirs to God's promise.

The New Covenant was born out of the sufferings and death of Christ at Calvary and his resurrection, revealing for all time the death and degradation that all persons suffer under tyranny and the oppression imposed by society. Those who perceived the death of Jesus as death for their sakes could break from the past; they received the power to work for new forms of life replacing and renewing old destructive forms.

The Old and the New Covenants have a secular context. They verify God's mighty acts *in the world*—in the defeat of the Egyptians, and in the binding together of a particular people. In the New Covenant in Christ there is the commandment to love God and the neighbor, and the liberating power of the love that never fails.

"By his great mercy we have been born anew to a living hope through the resurrection of Jesus Christ from the dead, . . . Once you were no people; but now you are God's people; once you had not received mercy, but now you have received mercy." (1 Peter 1:3; 2:9–10).

SUGGESTED APPROACHES TO CHAPTER 1

Three perplexing questions are before us as we analyze our times:

1. For what purpose do we believe in God and his Son Jesus Christ?
2. How do we make clear to the world that we have this belief?
3. How do we perceive what God is doing in the world?

To read the signs of the times as members of the Christian community we need both *theological reflection* and *sociological imagination:* the ability to sense the large social ethical consequences of our personal decisions and actions, and to see the personal tragedies and hurts which are at the heart of social issues. Without reflection and analysis we are apt to get cynical about our efforts, and think that large social issues are quite outside our sphere of action or accountability. Purely personal problems like mental illness have their roots in society, and cannot be resolved without social change—reforms in treatment, greater public concern. Likewise the outcome of the war in Indochina or the SALT talks (Strategic Arms Limitation Treaty) will affect the personal lives of millions and generations unborn.

Two sessions of at least ninety minutes length will be needed to begin to assess the state of society. This first session could be the *first stage* of a DO-IT-YOURSELF ANALYSIS of the state of society to be used to sensitize church people to what is happening around them.

There are several ways to get into the discussion of societal change and the Christian's response—moving out from personal faith to concern for and outreach to others:

1. Use the following opinionaire to provide "feedback" and individual reactions to the five statements on the previous pages. (The opinionaire can be mimeographed and distributed, or written on a large sheet of newsprint, with the participants raising their hands to indicate their opinions.)

Opinionaire (Please check the reactions below which are most like your views):

__I agree with most or all of the statements and believe they are accurate "signs of the times."

__Most of the statemnts are too negative and gloomy to be worth discussing.

__The statements accurately describe our times but they make me feel afraid and unwilling to face what is ahead.

__The statements challenge us to wake up to a new age.

__Statements like these represent God's judgment upon this world and its sin.

__Statements like these represent God's action in the world.

__The statements make me very angry. Why can't we keep things as they were?

2. Have group members list and discuss the changes they have seen personally in the community, family, church, region.

- Have these been the result of technological development?
- Expand this idea of "future shock" and apply it to your community. In what respects is it looking toward the future; is it blocking change?

3. Ask a group of students to describe *what young people are looking for*. How would they answer the question: What should be changed in this community? Our modern world? Invite a grandparent to moderate or to comment; old people and young people have a mutual need for each other. A coalition of these two "powerless" groups could give both a new power base. Between them there may be only a negligible "generation gap," or none at all.

4. Divide into small working parties to dig in on what signs of the times group members may be able to discern.

- What signs do you look for?

- *Why* are members of the Christian community called to look for signs—respond to signs? Do they do this as individuals? as church officers? as an evangelism committee? a social action group?

5. Discuss what group members think God is doing in the world. If God is acting, what should Christians do in response? Further reading of secular materials? See that God's work in the world is understood? Further Bible reading? Follow-up action?

In the second session on Chapter 1 there could be these approaches:

1. Extended Bible study at the opening or closing of the session. Small working groups should read and comment on particular Bible references, letting "the Word" get through to each participant. References in the Old and New Testaments which show the relationship between *Faith* and *Justice* may be cited, read and discussed: (a) The Ten Commandments, which command reverence for God and concern for neighbor; the chapters in Exodus describing the giving of the law; (b) Jesus' emphasis on the Deuteronomic code; (c) Jesus's reference to Isaiah 61:1,2 to identify himself in Luke 4:16–20; (d) 1 John 3: 18–16 suggest-

ing the style of life of the faithful Christian community.

In Ecclesiastes, for example, there is a radical, questioning mood, very similar to the mood of the young who are caught up in the tragedy of the drug culture. Kóheleth, the English spelling of a Hebrew word for preacher or teacher, speaks to *our times:* "Why is there suffering?" "Why should I go on living?" What about the first chapter of this strange book? "For in much wisdom is much vexation, and he who increases knowledge increases sorrow." Is there any ultimate meaning in life? Ecclesiastes offers us the challenge of searching for truth, the reality of truth in the full range of human experience and the search for meaning in the concrete events of daily life.

2. Continue the analysis begun in the first session—probing such matters as:

- Changes in the church—local congregation and beyond.
- Changes in family life—divorce, women's liberation, revolt of youth.
- Changes in population—age, race, social class.
- Evidences of economic growth or decline—new plants, closing of plants, dis-

placement of workers, effects of automation, the exodus of the young to find jobs.

- Changes in education—cultural life.
- Most critical problems—who is aware of these?
- What distinctly new things are happening?
- Overall characteristics of your community—industrial, suburban, branch-office town, company-town, conservative, liberal, dominated by unions or John Birch Society?

3. Try to describe concrete situations or experiences that give human beings a sense that there is a God. How do such situations or experiences help us to express concern for our neighbors? How does belief in God actually function in guiding us in decisions about such issues as welfare reform or equal opportunity employment?

4. Think of possible options for action in preparation for subsequent sessions. The group may want to assign a task force to work on this. Specific suggestions and examples are given in Chapters 2 and 4.

Examples: A suburban action center; a consultation on the Future for Human Beings in a World Dominated by Science-

Based Technology (modeled after the study launched by the National Council of Churches and Union Theological Seminary and a similar consultation held by the World Council of Churches in Geneva during the summer of 1970); a Women's Liberation Task Force to establish contact with the liberation movement and consider the status of women in the churches; a local community institute on racism; analysis of the effects of mass media and human communication on opinions and behavior of church members.

chapter

·2·

WHERE IS THE CHURCH?

The Christian churches have entered the seventies caught between the extremes that have deeply divided American society. Few denominations have escaped a sharp decline in members and in financial support. Most have experienced a crisis-type quandary about the future. No ecclesiastical immunity has protected them from the stormy divisions that have shaken other institutions, including the universities, the medical societies and the Welfare establishment.

Engagement in "radical social action," especially for radical justice, peace and a humanized open society has been thought to be the principal cause for dissension and decline in financial support. But almost as often the *lack* of social involvement is cited as a major cause for decline in interest on the part of young people. Dieter Hessel in *Reconciliation and Conflict*[1] believes that we are in the midst of "a complex controversy that has been building for some time and is not likely to end soon. . . . One [dissenting] group charges that the church is caught in an unholy alliance with political activism, . . . Others find the church to be so overweight from feeding herself that she may die soon." Today, as in the past, a majority of church members pay little attention to the debates swirling around national denominational offices. The church is simply not at the center of life for many of the laity, nor is it on their list of priorities. The annual Gallup Poll on organized religion indicates that 75 percent of the American people are of the opinion that the church is losing its influence.

The facts are that there is an exodus from the churches. Protestant ministers are leaving their ministries in increasing

[1] Dieter T. Hessell, *Reconciliation and Conflict: Church Controversy Over Social Involvement* (Philadelphia: The Westminster Press, 1969). Used by permission.

numbers. Roman Catholic priests and members of religious communities are leaving their churches and their religious orders to live in the world, marry and witness to the gospel in entirely secular vocations. The large centralized boards and agencies of the Protestant churches, which built new churches and financed new mission projects, are being reduced in scale or replaced by local and regional mission efforts. The big bureaucracies of the mainline denominations are rapidly dismantling because of the "budget squeeze," and withholding of funds for national programs which are deemed "too liberal." Tent-making ministries are growing, and may well be the life-style of the clergy of the future. Some ministers are leaving their parishes for secular jobs. They preach and administer the sacraments, but they no longer depend upon congregational giving for their salaries. The decline in church support raises a wide range of stewardship questions: Are we to be caught up in the death of our own institutions? Should the institutional church be saved? How can it be renewed? Do the changes in the modern world demand new kinds of Christian obedience? Or is it enough to do what has always been done?

Controversy in the churches is not new. Out of turmoil and conflict have come renewal and reformation—in the past. As an example, historians describe the Fundamental-Modernist controversy of fifty years ago that forced members of the churches to reexamine their faith in light of burgeoning scientific thought. But what is happening now seems to many to be of a deeper nature.

Contemporary theology and biblical study point up God's continuing activity in the world. There are specific changes, events and forces in society today which are creating new elements, raising new challenges, releasing new energies and determining new human responses. And because we live in one global social system, what happens in one sector of society affects all the rest.

The following events have profoundly stirred and shaken local congregations as well as great ecumenical assemblies:

1. *The Black Power movement and the rise of a powerful, articulate, ecumenical body of black clergy and laity.* The National Committee of Black Churchmen is an organization of black men and women who have come together across denominational lines, outside

of organized religion, for the purpose of exercising political influence both within the institutional structure of the churches and within the structures of the secular society; and to develop and interpret a theology of liberation, a *black* theology. NCBC provides leadership for the empowerment of the black community through larger and more effective use of the power, prestige and resources of the American religious establishment. In its formative period in 1968, NCBC was composed almost exclusively of clergy from the various denominations, black and white. Today it includes ordained and unordained persons from a wide spectrum of faiths, social classes, political persuasions and points of view. Among its members are also Mexican-Americans and Puerto Rican minorities. The founders of NCBC affirm the ideals of justice, freedom and well being and proclaim a theology of black liberation, seeking to plumb the human condition of black people in the light of God's revelation in Jesus Christ, so that the black community can clearly see that the gospel is commensurate with the achievement of black humanity. Black theology is a theology of "blackness," the affirmation of black humanity that emancipates black people from white racism, thus providing authentic freedom for both white and black people.[2]

[2] Position Paper authorized by the Executive Committee, October 10, 1969. Used by permission.

2. *The rise of La Raza Nueva and the affirmation of cultural pluralism.* This ground swell movement of Mexican-American solidarity throughout the Southwest has joined in fellowship and nonviolent revolutionary action 200–300 civic, social, cultural, religious and political groups. The title, "La Raza" was borrowed from the countries south of the Rio Grande, where it connotes a new family of men, composed of the original inhabitants of the Americas, the Indians and all other people, who, since the time of Columbus have come to the New World in search of a new creation. "La Raza" means "the human race" and points to the human values needed to heal the current illness of our national way of life. La Raza Nueva dramatizes the plight of a disadvantaged minority, the rights to first-rate citizenship, and to share in the social, economic, educational and political opportunities guaranteed by the American democratic system. In La Raza Nueva Roman Catholics and Protestants work and witness together. Every significant nonviolent protest has clergymen in its midst, to work for its advancement.[3]

3. *The world-wide rebellion and protest of youth and the serious effort of many to build a counter-culture.* The protest of youth against the values and life-styles established

---

[3] *La Raza Yearbook.* Used by permission.

by their parents is world-wide, and what began as a university campus revolt is now taking root in many high schools. Young people have put together their own highly effective networks for organizing, interacting and communicating. Where black students have pressed for black studies and charters of students' rights, Mexican-American youth are confronting school boards with demands for bi-lingual classes, challenging the repressive tactics of the police. With sleeping bags and underground news sheets they are ready to travel anywhere, and do. In less than a decade an incredible intellectual transformation is taking place. Peaceful demonstrations on campus are now accepted almost everywhere. The collection of money for social causes, recruiting of students for political activity, co-ed dormitories, open enrollment, Black Studies courses are now widely considered legitimate. The views of the radical students about the war in Southeast Asia, the war-related research operations of the university have combined to influence many youth and succeed in radicalizing a great majority. Mass media and rightist politicans have viewed the confrontations and the new student left as dangerous and terrorist, thus polarizing students and educators and failing to recognize that we have reached the end of an era when we could expect that successive generations of young people would follow parental patterns and "settle down" in the life-style of their parents as soon as they reach 35 or 40 years. This aspect of the new age has shaken church families all over the country, and even the most traditional church-related college and youth groups.

4. *The growth of Pentecostal-Fundamentalist movements.* An increasing number of persons, young and old, seek escape from the whirl of change and the agony of uncertainty by dependence on new forms of fundamentalism. "Speaking in tongues" and waiting for the Spirit engage a growing number of church members who are usually in church on Sundays but in their special prayer group during the week. Roman Catholics as well as Protestants claim to have found spiritual renewal and communication, even ecstasy, in Pentecostal revivalism. Many Jews have joined, affirming that Pentecostal faith is a fulfillment of Judaism. The dedicated ring door bells, distribute tracts, teach others the signs of the Second Coming. Crowds attend the services of healing, attesting to the power of prayer and the laying on of hands.

While attendance and membership decline in the mainline churches, the Jesus Movement seems to be everywhere, attracting young people reared in strictly religious homes as well as under suburban agnosticism. It turns on the disillusioned student radicals who have given up on politics, and the acid heads tired of tripping from one nightmare to the next. The cadres of adult evangelists who run the Jesus communes (or Christian homes) and raise funds for Jesus tracts, buttons and bumper stickers are spreading the Word with zeal, preaching doomsday and the coming of the rapture. Analysts of the movement are concerned about its apolitical, other-worldly stance, and also about the long-term effects on thousands of lonely freaked-out kids. Some critics have pointed to the possibility of capture and use of the Jesus People by right wing politicians and their affluent supporters.

5. *The demands of the Third World for liberation and a liberation theology.* The people of the Third World continue to challenge Protestant and Roman Catholic missionary efforts. Despite shifts in mission strategy and the wide-scale development of indigenous ministries, some churches overseas are still trapped in the institutional violence and neo-colonialism of the past. They still depend on American funds raised in the United States. Their leaders have been taught that their ancient cultural forms and history are "pagan," and in the process of becoming "Christianized" they have also become "westernized," thus destroying their own cultural-tribal roots and history.

From the Third World certain prophetic groups in Latin America, for example, are saying "no" to the North American forces which they believe depersonalize man, make him a compulsive consumer, neutralize his economic independence and also his independence of judgment. They are radically criticizing the American consumer society and rejecting it for the Third World. The prophets of the Third World are also questioning the basic assumptions on which the churches of the West have evangelized the Third World, and are calling for some rapprochement between Christianity and the other great religions of the world, looking to a wholly new concept of ecumenicity.[4]

As these powerful forces create further change in the world, where do we stand as members of the Christian community? Most of us are caught in a complex web of conflicting commitments (family vs. job; family vs. neighborhood pressure), responsibilities, yearnings, anxieties and hopes.

Most of us are caught between the old world and the new. Our commitments, personal relationships, ways of living make it hard for us to fit into new situations. Yet our survival may require living and wor-

[4] Notes from *An Introduction to a Theology of Liberation,* by Rev. Gustavo Perez Ramirez, 1971, CICOP Conference.

shiping in radically different ways. In our personalities we represent the persistence of tradition and the fear of the unknown. Can the institutional church be a supportive, challenging community to sustain us in the transition?

Many church members join the church for highly individualized reasons, and to receive individualized satisfactions or dissatisfactions: I like the minister, the location. Seldom do we hear of people joining because there is corporate congregational scope for work and witness, or because they seek a community of understanding to keep them alive in a dehumanizing society.

Many of us are searching for this community of understanding to help us realize wholly and fully our true humanity. To live through and in the midst of change we need to establish sustaining relationships with others for mutual support and sharing of burdens and joys. Few of us can make it on our own! So this question is before us: Where do we find this supportive community? In the church?

THEOLOGICAL REFLECTION

Freedom and justice are described in the scriptures in the dynamics of a new relationship. The Covenant of God with his people and its renewal in Jesus Christ is not a legal contract but a promise of total commitment of God and man to each other and to all others. We are familiar with the many scriptural descriptions of the early church. The Apostle Paul writes to the Ephesians about head-body relationships, all parts of the body knit firmly together growing toward Christ, the head. According to Christ's promise, he is not only where "two or three" are gathered in his name (Matthew 18:20) but also in the least of his brothers, the hungry and the naked, the sick and the imprisoned (Matthew 25:31 ff). Contrary to this scriptural teaching, our own contemporary experience ties the church to a particular building, a much loved pastor, a memorial to a rich member and much less often to a community of believers.

In our theological reflection and social analysis, we look at some questions that are disturbing clergy and laity, even polarizing the churches and destroying community:

- Does religion have to do with the real world where people live—the world of politics, race, sex, art, drama—or not?
- Ought the churches and synagogues to

take sides in the struggle for peace, racial justice and the ending of poverty—or remain neutral?

- Should sermons and prayers deal with the anguished world of power, nonwhite and white—or not?
- Should the church seek to change men's hearts only and trust that they will "take" the gospel into the world to change it? Or should the church also seek to change those political, economic and social structures that condemn large numbers to poverty, ignorance and disease, generation after generation?

To have faith in God is to perceive and take part in the dynamics of hope, hope of becoming fully human persons in a fully human society. How does the church become the supportive community that enables us to be fully human?

We believe that a supportive community is a gift of the Holy Spirit, but it also requires our human response, and becomes manifest to the members of the community when these elements are present:

- When the supportive community is reading the signs of the times, and interpreting what is going on in the world to its members and to others. In many parts of the world Christians are discovering their role as "discerners," understanding, for example, the people's struggle against oppression as a "sign." When the supportive community is demonstrating in its own life its oneness, through the love of Christ and love of neighbor, as a community of acceptance, forgiveness, judgment and grace. Members of the body can mature and grow in their own unique humanity, as they grow together and toward Christ their Lord.

- When the supportive community reminds its members who they are, to whom they are accountable and of the ultimate consequences of their acts and behavior.
- When the supportive community helps to determine goals and values for living—what values remain of the past, which shall be changed and what new values are needed for a new age.
- When the supportive community can be a reconciling force, wiping away estrangements and helping members to take off the masks they wear. When there is openness there is always the

possibility of new insight, the discovery of new directions, new kinds of relationships. Without openness we run the risk of false and arrogant pride in our own opinions. The least we can do is to listen to others and keep communications open.

- When the supportive community has become identified with the poor and oppressed. The suffering of the poor has as its purpose the creation of a new society. Our Christian faith calls upon the privileged to join in the suffering, to *become those* who suffer and thus participate as the builders of the new community—witnesses to God's power and love.

Archie Hargraves wrote in *Renewal,* June 1969, that: "The question is no longer how Riverside Church, or any other church can minister to the world. That question is absolutely of no interest at all, and of no importance. The question really is: Where is the real show going on? Where is God speaking now? Where is God being heard and where is he being obeyed? Where is he being experienced? And whose side is he on? Is he taking sides? And who are the people who witness to God—who point him out and detail what he is doing—even though they may be mistaken, in order to awaken those who are oppressed and get them to do something about a change in their condition? What are they doing to structure this experience? What are they doing to structure God's voice? What are they doing to evangelize in terms of a new living experience of God?

"Now the Holy Spirit blows where it will, and it seems to have bypassed the church institutions. . . . What then is the role of (the) church . . . To recognize that there is this freshness, this new source of discovery, this new source of revelation. And we've got to open ourselves to a new kind of experience, a new kind of rustling of the wind by God, the whirlwind of the Lord."

APPROACHES TO CHAPTER 2

1. Set up listening teams to close the communications gap between young people and "those over thirty." What are young people saying, and why? Who really listens to the kids? What young people are thinking, and why, must be understood by adults in the church and in society. Without the young can there be a future? Grandparents and/or older people not related by kinship

often have time and opportunity to establish rapport with the young. If interaction can be achieved, rewards are great for both groups. More often than we may realize, young people and old people are drawn to each other for mutual support. A surprising number of young people are preparing for careers related to the aged and gerontology. Young lawyers and community organizers, for example, are probing the big unexplored morass of health law and health services for the elderly at the Law School of the University of Pennsylvania. On the east coast, working out of New York, Philadelphia and Washington, there is a small but solid coalition of students and retirees working together for peace and justice. Both groups are powerless in our society, but together they are developing a new base of power and influence. Information and understanding are also needed locally about the "Jesus Freaks," and the young people who are turning to Eastern religions.

2. Analyze your own congregation and its corporate influence in the world. How does your church stand on urban problems, war and peace, civil rights, poverty and welfare? Who is concerned about the effects of injustice? What are the chief concerns of

the officers of your church? What do the members think the church should be and do? A survey by Jeffrey K. Hadden, author of *The Gathering Storm in the Churches,* identifies the growing gap between the clergy and the laity and the significant differences among ministers with respect to social outlook as well as doctrine.

The annual Gallup Poll on Organized Religion may provide other statistics to ponder and discuss. What percentage of the members of your congregation believe that the influence of the church is declining? Growing? Holding its own?

By the use of the following check list (or one your group prepares) choose what you think would be the option for your church in facing the possibility of decline in the next 5–10 years. Then try polling members of your church during some church gathering, for instance after Sunday worship. Check one or more of statements such as these:

1. Don't worry about the future; continue the present type of ministry.
2. Appoint a task force to study causes for decline and recommend new forms of ministry and strategy.
3. Call a meeting of the congregation and

ask representatives from each grouping of the church to present some plans for their future.

4. Set up calling committees or visitation teams to contact every member, particularly those members who do not come regularly.

5. Plan a vigorous evangelistic program to reach persons who are not affiliated with local churches.

6. Plan and conduct new series of mid-week or Sunday night discussions followed by a small but well-trained action team moving out into the community.

7. Let the present church die, keep in close touch with the members and rebuild new structures with the people who "drop out."

8. Set up a new worship committee to radicalize forms of Sunday morning worship.

As the group discusses these options and what they have chosen, press for agreement on what they think would be effective in creating new interest in the gospel and in the mission of Christians. Could decline be stopped? Reversed? Where are the frontiers?

3. Develop a statement of purpose and mission. With the same working parties set up to probe the first chapter, make an inven-

tory of the issues which you consider most crucial for the church to act on. Ask one or two people to draft a statement of purpose and mission to be approved by the whole group. Work on strategy to get church officers and members of the congregation to consider the statement or to draft a statement of their own, describing what they believe to be the mission and purpose of their church. To avoid being put down as "meddlers" it may be important to enlist key church members as allies even before a study-action group begins its work.

4. Declare a moratorium on business as usual. In an historic church in New Jersey the congregation and all the existing church organizations (including choir, church school, women's groups) voted to suspend all regular meetings and organizational business for a year. The only exceptions were Sunday worship and monthly meetings of the church board. Purpose of the moratorium: To release time, energy and talents of lay leadership to experiment with new forms of worship, association and mission, and to reach agreement about new frontiers for the seventies. Members report a year of excitement and *creative stress*. A planning group and several task forces

(including nonmembers from the community): (a) probed community needs, the needs and concerns of the members; (b) developed a skill bank of members' talents; (c) analyzed the relationship of members of the congregation to community decision-making (who was on school board, planning commission, state university faculty, RCA research, etc.). Sunday worship services expanded to day-long church and world discussions. New goals were set, new structure devised to achieve them. At least half of the members participated in a thorough analysis of what was most urgent for the congregation to do.

5. Experiment with new forms of worship and ways to proclaim and celebrate the good news. Some innovations can be made from time to time without making drastic changes, for example: Intercessory prayers in which the petitions of members are voiced, dialogue sermons, scripture readings interwoven with readings from daily papers, communion-in-the-round, antiphonal readings with congregational participation—all the women, the children, the aged, the visitors standing in turn and reading appropriate commentary and confession. Some churches are constantly pro-

claiming the gospel in fresh, exciting ways, using the talents of their members and affirming the "living Word of God" in contemporary human situations and forms of communication.

6. Seek new allies and coalitions for action. Most suburbs are strongholds of noninvolvement and private pursuits of tranquility. Escape from urban problems is the objective that few will admit. Whatever action occurs in suburban areas is usually engineered by a few, and aimed to perpetuate the escape from the problems of the city: a zoning fight to keep out low-income housing or industry, a campaign for a separate school district. The challenge is to involve white middle class people in terms of their own self-interest and personal satisfactions, across denominational and racial barriers. Suburban churches linked with the decision-making secular groups of suburbs have organized suburban action centers for these and other goals:

- To tackle white racism that is built in our white institutions—confronting the injustice in our present systems of welfare, medical service, the courts.
- To provide human and national resources to aid indigenous groups in the

city to organize to work on their own agenda for change.

- To engage in continuous efforts to sensitize and "conscientize" (borrowed from Latin America) white suburbanites, working to involve and change various vocational groups.
- To promote reform of political processes, making these more responsive to the real needs of people—and taking effective political action—including motivation to run for political office.
- To set up dialogue groups, "hot-line" referral services, legal counseling.

7. Use drama and the arts. Drama has been the principal means of communication and confrontation in two suburban action centers. A small artists-in-residence theater with a more or less permanent group of players is related to the center. Visiting players and drama students come from time to time to write, discuss and present plays. A small touring company takes short, provocative plays to local churches and meetings, and presents summer theater in the streets and in playgrounds. The purpose of the drama is to spark emotional response to human situations portraying human need and conflict. Drama inter-

prets the black experience to white people and exposes prejudice and racism. Wherever the touring company goes the interest of the players is "to raise the issues" so that new patterns of response, thinking and behavior can be "tried for size."

A group of Mexican-American players have developed great skill and sensitivity with socio-drama and improvisations. In East Los Angeles they organized a traveling troop to follow the stream of migrant farm workers as they moved up the California valleys. In the evenings members of the drama group led informal singing and moved into discussions of the problems migrants live with. The problems became situations for improvisation and role-playing, and players and audience acted out the problems, became articulate about them, and ready to try new approaches and possible solutions. The director demonstrated that drama, socio-drama, psycho-drama, can be a powerful tool for organizing and empowering groups for community action.

In any or all approaches to the building of the supportive, redemptive community, we must struggle to make the oneness of the community clearly visible to ourselves and to others outside the camp.

However great the strain of dissension may be, the church has the potential for being one place in society where opportunities for human interaction are *always* possible, where there is openness and the capacity to listen to the other side. No human problem or injustice or sin should be outside the supportive community's care and concern; no masks should be needed when there is love and forgiveness. It is within the oneness of our faith that God's reconciling power is explicitly acknowledged, and the history of his work among men in Jesus Christ remembered and celebrated.

chapter 3

INSTITUTIONAL RENEWAL

This chapter deals with institutions established by church groups to meet human needs, and with the effects of change upon these institutions. It further suggests how many of our church-related institutions—schools, hospitals, community centers, homes for the aged, for example—might be renewed, retooled, even recycled with new life and purpose.

The Institutional Crisis

All institutions in our society have been subjected to great strain in this period of rapid change; our church institutions have not escaped the forces that have shaken universities, public schools and secular health and welfare agencies. Even the United States Marine Corps revised its manuals and eased regulations about the traditional crew cut.

New needs and forces for change have overwhelmed many church institutions. Some have been kept alive only by endowments and their history even though the need for which they were organized no longer exists. Institutions have a peculiar ability to survive. By their nature they tend to be self-perpetuating. One familiar survival technique is to engulf the challenging elements, as the oyster does the irritating bits of sand. Demands for change may be heard by institutional heads, referred to "top-level" conferences, assigned to subcommittees for study, analyzed in working papers to be discussed in endless rounds that can delay action and actual change almost indefinitely.

The neighborhood center of old Central Church is a classic illustration of "containment." It was set up nearly seventy years ago to reach an Italian immigrant population. Several well-to-do church families made it their favorite charity. Long after the Italians had moved out and the area was almost completely black and Puerto Rican, the white Italian-speaking head worker continued to live at the center, and have an occasional spaghetti supper for Italian mothers and grandmothers who came miles from their suburban homes for a reunion. The church families continued to pay her modest salary and buy the supper tickets. When occasionally questions were asked about the use of the building by the immediate community, the Center Board would hold several open meetings, appoint another study committee, and bury the recommendations. The staff would take the matter under advisement and do nothing. Deacons, trustees and concerned church members had long discussions about what the Center should be doing. Only the death of the head worker at the age of 80 broke the continuity. After her death the property was sold to a "storefront" evangelist, and funds invested in an ecumenical center.

Some Central Church members despaired about the passing of the old benevolent order of doing good for others. Some found it hard to face the realities of new human situations (slum housing, fighting gangs, squalor and misery) and became frustrated and weary, with little energy to begin anew. Others in the church welcomed the shaking of the old foundations, seeing the disarray both judgment and grace, the breaking open of old structures to permit new life to begin.

Agents of Change and Reconciliation

Although it is popular today to put down institutions as archaic remnants of the past, they are a potential source of new power and influence for our churches; their tangible assets—land, buildings, human resources, a continuity of concern and service—could be deployed in new ways to meet emerging needs. Institutions constitute a common meeting ground on which conservatives and liberals can stand together. Institutions can be the arena where a comprehensive strategy is worked out by the people who are concerned. Some will choose the direct service approach, ministering in many ways to needy people. Others will choose the organizer-social activist approach. Within an institutional program all of their efforts could be important and interrelated.

If church institutions are to be "common ground" for mission it is necessary to assess the new human situation to which the church is called to minister. Many institutions, schools for freedmen and slaves, hospitals for Indians and Mexican-Americans, for example, were established by concerned, well-meaning whites *for* nonwhites. They were truly pioneering efforts, requiring sacrifice and hardship, but they were run on a paternalistic basis upon the assumption that *white* values, standards, program goals were best for everybody and that everybody wanted them.

Today the demand for participation, full sharing in decisions and governance is everywhere. It is not a demand to be enrolled or given therapy; it is a demand to run things in ways that affirm the values and aspirations not of middle class, educated whites, but of poor whites, blacks, Chicanos, Puerto Ricans, Indians, the people who have been the objects of the benevolence of white churchmen.

The passage of the 1964 Civil Rights Act, the 1965 Voting Rights Act, and legislation related to the War on Poverty, raised the expectations of minorities, but those expectations have not been fulfilled. The Report of the National Advisory Commission on Civil Disorders and other data show that segregation and poverty have worsened in many areas of greatest concentration of black and Spanish-speaking people. The gulf between the affluent and the poor gets wider.

Black Power advocates see integration more as a by-product resulting from powerful social and political action than as a self-conscious goal to which everything else *must* be subordinated. Militant organization for social action has steadily increased among other minority groups, such as the Spanish-American poor and the American Indians, as well as blacks. The emergence of Black Power, as a strategy to enhance pride, cultural identity and political and economic self-determination, has stimulated grass roots community organization in ghettos and confronted white liberals with the challenge to surrender the initiative and leadership of the struggle for justice to black people.

White racism has been given significant official status as the root cause of our nation's race relations problems by the Report of the National Advisory Commission on Civil Disorders, and such sociological studies as that by Glock and Stark have revealed its entrenchment in the church.

In the midst of tensions, churches and church institutions face events and forces which cannot be predicted or controlled, least of all by white middle class groups. New concepts of "welfare," "service," "participation," are being proclaimed in every quarter. The challenge should be clear: The institutions still related to the churches represent a new base of power for minority groups. The clamoring of people in the Third World and the ghettos and barrios of the United States can be the creative context for institutional change. Middle class white congregations could have a decisive part in the liberation of minorities by "freeing" their institutions from all paternalistic governance and committing them to the people. Land, buildings and people could be brought into the vanguard of institutional liberation in the United States and all over the world where institutions were established by the missionary movement.

THEOLOGICAL REFLECTION

Outreach to the neighbor is essential to the health of the religious community. It is also the motivation for our concern for justice, our stewardship of our lives and our possessions. Without commitment to others, churches, like all human groups, become ingrown, selfish enclaves, ceasing to do the redemptive work of Christ. Contemporary theologians are showing us that the world writes the church's agenda. As the church responds to the conflicts, pressures and changes in the world, the church too is tempted to seek her own status and power, taking pride in numbers and works. Yet all of our efforts are provisional, temporary, subject to God's judgment.

As people of faith we must experience the tearing down and the building up of our cherished institutions, sharing as we do the experience of death and resurrection. Both Jesus and Paul destroyed what the Temple had come to stand for. With the gospel, the structure of Jewish piety and practice was broken. (Galatians 1 and 2; Acts 15 to 28). In the New Covenant community legalism and tradition gave way to love.

In Christian churches there is talk every Sunday about "stewardship" usually in terms of *members giving* to the institutional church—money, time, talents for the church. Some white and nonwhite theologians are attempting to show that "stewardship" also refers to what the institutional church does about its own "stewardship," and how it uses the time, talents, land, buildings and money that are the assets of its institutions.

The stewards which the churches have appointed to watch over their funds—treasurers, finance and investment committees, have generally followed market place standards of fiscal accountability and "dollar yield." This concept of fiscal responsibility is slowly changing. In the last five years some church bodies have adopted guidelines for the investment of church funds and the use of investment capital for social benefit, recognizing that investment funds are instruments of mission, and must always be subject to decisions based on ethical, theological and social considerations.

The young theologians involved in the Jonathan's Wake movement have written a position paper on American Church Stewardship,[1] stating five mandates based on biblical authority, the Word which finds its full expression in the person and ministry of the Christ, Jesus, toward which it points and which it reflects:

---

[1] *American Church Stewardship: Toward a Biblical Analysis,* by Jonathan's Wake. A position paper prepared for the mobilization to end the war in the churches, New York City, November 12–13, 1970.

1. *The ethics of the Kingdom should, in so far as possible, be the ethics of the Body of Christ.* Paul recognizes difficulty in living out this ethic of beatitude, love and mutual sharing of the Spirit's gift, but, particularly when the church is divided and in need of new life, he exhorts the members to recall the Cross and Resurrection, those events which transform the world and inaugurate the Kingdom proclaimed by the prophets and incarnate in Jesus . . . The spirit of Christ—of peace, of caring not for the morrow, of traveling light, of reversing the roles of the rich and poor—is more to be cultivated than a pure profit motive which leads to church investment in the creation of destruction.

2. *The heart of Jesus' vision of the future involves a last judgment at which the material aid and comfort given one's fellow man is the primary basis for inclusion in the kingdom.* This is the clear indication of Matthew 25 but even a less literal approach to the word would see in Jesus the fulfillment of the prophetic criticism of profit, in so far as profit is the instrument of another's misfortune. Given the history of the world since Christ's resurrection, it could well be argued that the world is being suffered to exist until such time as the church has received the message of Matthew 25. The implication for the stewardship of the institutional church seems clear in any case: Our resources should be

used to meet the needs of those who lack our advantages.

3. *Within the church there should be generosity to poorer members.* Such a statement may seem paternalistic to modern ears, but it is important to see that the church today is under the same mandate as the church in the time of Paul. Paul exhorts the churches to mutual responsibility for the upbuilding of the whole. Our very system of segregation by denomination, race and nation means that the only way to begin a process of mutual responsibility is to recognize that our churches themselves operate on standards which inhibit the fulfillment of this mandate. Few white American churchmen would deny in principle that there are many, many poor and needy church members both in and beyond the United States. But equally few would respond readily to the notion that the billions poured into religious facilities ought more properly to be shared with those less fortunate brothers and sisters in Christ. They must now see that the failure to share wealth within the church is one cause of schism which can only be remedied by restitution.

4. *Jesus stood against the church being a corporation.* The only confrontation of Jesus with the religious institution on a financial issue was his expulsion of the money-changers and vendors from the Jerusalem Temple. We are aware from Mark that this event

sealed his execution. And we know that his reason for doing what may have been a violent deed was quite specific. He said the use of the religious facility for business had made it "a den of thieves" and thus it could not be what it was intended to be: "a house of prayer for all nations." Note that Jesus was not simply saying that involvement in secular business taints the religious institution; he is saying too that disengagement from such business would restore the institution to its primary function—to be a house of prayer.

5. *Disputes within the church are to be solved by the sincere efforts of disputants to settle their differences within the church and not in the world.* In Paul there is a strong suggestion that disputes of any sort should be settled within the church rather than in courts of law. For this reason we believe that the dispute concerning the legitimacy of present official stewardship should be settled by honestly acknowledging that it exists and taking steps to create a way to solve it consistent with the need for unity within the church. Accordingly we have made our first effort one of seeking the ordained ministers on investment committees to act as interpreters and intermediaries between grass roots church members and the small group of men who have largely determined present stewardship practices. . . .

As a final biblical observation, let it be proclaimed that Jesus died and was raised to give new life to all men including the rich young ruler who rejected his suggestion to go and sell all he had and follow him.

SUGGESTED APPROACHES TO CHAPTER 3

Outreach to neighbor through institutional ministries should bring together members of congregations and the persons served by our institutions. The commitment of the supportive community to the neighbor requires far more than pledges of financial support. Most white middle class congregations need to be sensitized by personal contact and participation in the sufferings of those whose life experiences expose most sharply the failings of society. Alienated, impoverished minorities need to be personally aware that they have advocates to join them in seeking justice and freedom. Church renewal and institutional renewal can be reinforcing experiences.

1. Organize small visiting teams of two to four church members to establish contact with the church-related institutions in your area. Fruitful relationships can begin informally. By careful observation and

friendly visits with staff and persons involved in the program, much can be learned about our institutions—their goals, how they are administered, whom they serve and how well they are meeting human needs. Visits can be made in: (a) hospitals, particularly noting the clinics and wards; (b) retirement homes and nursing homes, noting evidences of neglect and isolation; (c) neighborhood centers; (d) day care programs for children and the aged; (e) experiments in economic development, community organization. Visiting teams could include young people and older people from the congregation. To provide some continuity, teams may wish to work with a particular kind of institution—a hospital, home for aged. In preparation for the visits, teams should:

- Meet to plan schedules and how to begin.
- Work out questions to ask directors, residents, patients, users of services.
- Get all available material describing the institution: brochures, by-laws, financial statements.
- Discuss what to look for in observing program and administration goals. Who are served?

- Map plan for follow-up visits and ways to get more church members to participate.
- Work out reporting system to bring about interaction between congregation and institution.

It is impossible to generalize on what the visiting teams will turn up. But instances of neglect, mismanagement, safety hazards, faulty equipment, staff shortages, should be carefully noted and reported to the pastors and officers of local churches, diocese or Presbytery officers, state and/or local health and welfare officers. Churches that help to fund institutions should exercise "responsible oversight" of their programs, oversight meaning a continuing concern for the well-being of all persons served by the institution.

Here are fundamentals to watch for:

The general spirit and atmosphere. (Is it friendly, depressing, restrictive, excessively neat?)

The quality of human relationships—among staff members, relationship of director to subordinates and to users of services (patients, clients, group members, etc.).

Extent to which users of services have a

part in influencing or determining program and/or operation of institution.

Extent to which program is relevant to current needs, and responsive to new needs.

The philosophy of administration and policy-making—the functioning of the Board of Directors; who serves on Board? How are Board members elected? Are participants represented?

Participation in church-related institutions as volunteers, friendly visitors and interpreters provides important training and experience in dealing with community issues of health, education and welfare. For a society to be truly human and just there must be broad-based social awareness and concern. Church leaders must be prepared to deal with questions of public policy, social ethics and the larger public interest. The socially concerned and faithful church has a witness in community affairs, proclaiming the good news by its own example and in its advocacy of "the least of these," those who are oppressed, despised and neglected by society.

In its witness to the love of Christ and God's rule in human affairs the church-related institution would seem to have these roles:

- To provide leadership in setting new social goals for society.
- To plan processes which encourage institutional change to meet new needs.
- To demonstrate new, experimental forms of service, and models of governance.
- To set up criteria for evaluating adequacy of service.
- To be the advocate of neglected and despised minorities.

2. Pioneer with some new guidelines for institutions. Guidelines for institutional management are available from denominational, ecumenical and government sources. These should be carefully assessed. But there are other guidelines which are to be observed by the churches, which go beyond such matters as professional and licensing standards for staff, housekeeping, legal standards and codes for buildings and facilities. What we have in mind can be illustrated in terms of new concepts of ministries with older persons.

(a) *Social analysis of a new situation.*

One of the most striking aspects of modern society, in contrast to earlier and more primitive cultures, is the increased proportion of a population that can reasonably be assured of reaching a venerable age. In the United States, the percentage of older citizens has more than doubled during the past half century and at present is approaching a ratio of 1 to 10. In 1900 the average span of life was 43 years, today it is 73 years. By the end of this century the number of Americans 65 or over is expected to reach 32 million.

Modern science has succeeded in helping many more people reach an extended age; but as a society we have been remiss in giving meaning and fullness to the extra years. In spite of all that is being done in the area of geriatrics and gerontology, the aged in western society stand a good chance of becoming *forgotten* men and women, subjected to a life of idleness, loneliness and near poverty within this affluent society. Very likely, the older American will end his days in an institution. If he is fortunate, he will receive adequate physical care and even, perhaps, good psychosocial care; but chances are he will not.

Churches have been concerned about the aged and the infirm for many years. As the human life span has been extended well beyond the biblical three score and ten years and fewer and fewer families can care for their older members, we see more and more retirement homes and nursing facilities being provided, many by church groups. Homes for the elderly now constitute the largest category of church institutions. Analysis of the needs of the aged and the adequacy of these homes in meeting needs could be significant in planning and guiding changes in other institutions.

(b) *Philosophy of church bodies concerning ministries with older persons.*

It is said that a society is known by the way it treats its aged members. Our society is primarily youth-centered and moves old people aside as soon as they reach "retirement age." A significant majority of the twenty million Americans who are 65 years of age have difficulty in obtaining housing, medical care and food. By arbitrary retirement policies, old people are excluded from productive work and a respected place in society, and also from an adequate income. Our strong cultural bias against oldsters operates even in the institutions set up to meet their needs.

In retirement homes residents are usually regarded as children to be cared for, amused, kept safe and out of the way. With such disregard of their ability to think and plan they soon become children. Our institutions reflect the mindsets of society and often reinforce them.

In *The Aged Ill,* Dorothea Jaeger, retired nursing educator, and Leo Simons, anthropologist, reported their findings from an extensive analysis of the attitudes of administrators, nurses' aids, patients, and patients' families in more than 100 nursing homes, including church-related homes. Their observations are both illuminating and shocking. Most institutions deal with what the authors cite as *"instrumental needs"* (housing, nutrition, etc.) with little attention to the following *fundamental needs* that are typical of all aging persons:

(1) To live as long as possible, or at least until life's satisfactions no longer compensate for its privations or the advantages of death seem to override the burdens of life.

(2) To preserve and conserve one's energies and potentials, physical and otherwise, against depletion by rest, relaxation, recuperation, renewal of health.

(3) To safeguard and strengthen, wherever possible, one's skills and assets, the rights and prerogatives acquired earlier in life.

(4) To continue some pertinent participation in group affairs. Sharing of interests

and activities is preferred for its own sake, regardless of secondary gain therefrom, over sheer idleness on the part of the aged or indifference on the part of associates significant to them.

(5) Finally, to find a closure to one's life, when necessity calls for it, that has maximum prospects for an attractive and rewarding hereafter. Everywhere there appears a valued difference between dying in victory or at least with dignity and dying in defeat with degradation.

(c) *Self-determination and self-development.*

Ministry with older adults begins with older persons who should be engaged in their own self-development. The aged have the same essential rights and requirements which all possess: the right to maximum self-determination, privacy of person and thought and personal dignity. Infringement of these rights or the failure to provide facilities or programs for exercising them violates the person's rights as a human being. The goal of each form of service should be to maximize the independence of the older person, and extend opportunities for social interaction with others, particularly younger persons.

Many questions have been raised about the availability, the cost, the quality of care in retirement homes, and most recently about the exclusion of the elderly from the mainstream of life and other age groups. Many homes require large "founder's" fees for admission and cost from $300–500 per month in addition to the founder's fees. Residents have frequently given up their life savings for the "security" of living in an institution where they have no part in determining program or policy. Seldom are they given any voice in the administration or program direction of the homes regardless of their experience and competence in such matters. Thus the wisdom, creativity and resourcefulness of older adults and their potential contribution to the governance of their own institutions have been almost completely overlooked, and a flagrant paternalism prevails.

A militant group of retirees has organized and joined with other reformers in pressing for radical changes in the governing policies and operations of homes with: (1) residents having voting membership on governing boards and controlling votes on program councils; (2) institutions providing a great variety of out-of-residence services to older persons living in the community; (3) institutions providing services for the general population—day care for young children, literacy classes, tutoring service for teenagers, adult education to stimulate interaction with the community.

chapter

·4·

MINISTERS AND THEIR MINISTRIES

Another way to probe the meaning and interaction of faith and justice is to consider what we mean by ministry. Who are the ministers in our churches? The ordained clergy in charge of priestly rites and sacraments? What about the ministry of the *laos*, the people of God in the pews? If we accept the priesthood of all believers, how do the laity minister? By helping the pastor? By their own vocations in the world?

In the Greek, to minister is to be the servant. In the New Testament Christ himself is the *diakonos*, the son of man who came not to be served but to serve (Matthew

20:28; Mark 10:45). As the Christian community does the work of *diakonia* it actually serves the Lord, Jesus Christ. Where this great mystery is recognized, it is possible to serve others without paternalism, and to receive the gifts of love without embarrassment.

Earlier in this guide we discussed the need for a supportive community and some of its characteristics. Here we consider how the supportive community equips its members for ministry.

The priesthood of all believers has been universally preached throughout Christendom but all too rarely practiced. In theory all Christians are called by *vocation* to proclaim and demonstrate the love of Christ and neighbor whatever their *occupation* may be. But to many lay people, even devout churchgoers, there is a great gulf between the faith we profess and the work we do in the world. Many live in two separate worlds—the private world of piety and the public world of work and politics. Lay persons have frequently interpreted the doctrine in terms of individual morality and what they do individually to deal justly and honestly with others. What is different in this age is the concern of *groups of lay per-*

sons about the imperatives of the gospel, and their *corporate,* ethical responsibilities and opportunities to respond to what God is doing in the world.

Ministries of the Laity

While some congregations are worried about their diminishing numbers, lay people all over the world are getting together in small and large groups to consider the ethical-social demands of their vocations and the larger claims of their communities for justice. These gatherings take many forms. In every profession there is ferment, and motion for change. In the vigorous debate and conflict of views many are asking ultimate questions about goals and values to live by, the good life and the ethics of achieving it. Modern technology complicates the questions about human value by putting before us all kinds of ethical questions entirely new to the human race. Some are life-and-death issues of survival!

On October 1, 1968, the National Council of Churches began an extraordinary project consisting entirely of lay people—developed, led and funded by lay people in the churches—*Listening to Lay People.* In 23 different communities across the nation each group of lay persons was asked to work on this central question: *What should the institutional church do to help lay people do what they as responsible Christians should be doing in their occupational, political, social and other in-the-world relationships and responsibilities?*

Planning committees in each community chose and invited the members of the listening groups, selected "an issue" about which Christians should be concerned and which was also a critical issue in that locality. The community groups ranged in size from 13 to 31 and met from 12 to 18 hours. Each group prepared a report of the discussions and specific recommendations. The objective of the project: *To develop in the Christian church a new ministry through lay people to the institutions of the secular world.*

To achieve this objective it was necessary to try to discover how the barrier between "sacred" and "secular" can be overcome in practice so that all of life where Christian lay people live and work now becomes the arena for the church's ministry, not a ministry to lay people, but a ministry of the whole church to the world through lay people.

Traditionally the churches have responded to the idea of "ministry" in a traditional institutional way: by attempting to get more lay members to join the church and become involved in church activities, church school classes, dinners, church-centered service projects. So accustomed are the churches to this way that both lay people and the clergy find it hard to believe that the laity have anything to say *to* the church, or that the church would listen. The lay people in the "listening" project had the same difficulty. They discovered that they had a great deal to say *to* the church about the secular world where they lived, but they could not find direct answers to the central question: What should the institutional church do to help lay people with the responsibilities and relationships they have where they live and work?

The report as a whole developed from the 23 community groups can be summed up in these disturbing words: "The church has abandoned us." The lay people agreed that, "it seems imperative for Christians to gather in respect to our function in society. . . . Most of us are in great need of the kind of guidance which will help us to relate our faith to the jobs we hold, the power we exercise, the influence we bear, and to the decisions we help to make. . . . We cry out for such a ministry now! The very faith we possess creates our dilemmas, disturbs our conscience, and demands the resolution of inner and social conflicts. We need a supportive ministry from the church which can nourish our faith and help us take up our roles in secular society as Christians. The ministry of the church to the institutions of society begins in a ministry through lay people who make up these institutions."

Studies of Technology and the Future of Man and Society

Scientists, particularly biologists, technologists and planners in government and industry, are very anxious about the ultimate social consequences of their research. Many are facing deep and agonizing ethical problems which science alone cannot resolve. The average citizen has little awareness of the danger. Groups of scientists are getting together today as physicists did thirty years ago when they began working on nuclear fission.

The nuclear physicists then were in a similar moral dilemma, and could not disassociate themselves from the awesome consequences of their work. Einstein said after the war, "If I had known that the Germans would not succeed in constructing the atom bomb, I would never have lifted a finger." J. Robert Oppenheimer said that the physicists had known sin. As scientists they felt themselves to be inadequately equipped to make the judgments they were called to make. They held long discussions with those whom they thought might be better equipped—philosophers, theologians, politicians. They had crusades to Washington. In an attempt to openly discuss the problems of moral and political responsibility in the use of atomic energy they produced a journal, *The Bulletin of the Atomic Scientists,* in which they confessed their anxiety and sense of guilt. Politically they had two great objectives: the civilian control of atomic energy in the U.S., and the international control of atomic energy in the world. They succeeded in the first but not the second objective.[1]

The Pugwash Movement, so called from the name of the small town in Canada where the first meeting was held in 1957, was a nonofficial organization of physicists concerned about thermonuclear war and the risk of universal death. Pugwash Conferences prepared the way for test ban

[1] From *Anticipation,* June 1970, World Council of Churches. Used by permission.

treaties, and treaties on outer space and nonproliferation. It was because the scientists knew so much and were so aware of the moral issues that they were involved in the consequences of their discoveries.

The New Supportive Community

The pursuit of a new more human community has intrigued church people through the centuries. The monastic communities established by Roman Catholics in Europe and North America are probably the best known examples. The Iona Community in Scotland, Taizé in France are contemporary Protestant forms. These communities have a firm theological and economic base and have been able to provide for the material and spiritual needs of their members and reach out to serve others. The idea of cooperative living has been fostered by the Religious Society of Friends with a number of successful housing developments.

Today in the midst of heated discussions about cultural breakdown and scattered efforts to build a counter-culture which would be a human society, the dream of the New Jerusalem has a great deal of vitality.

A group of 70 to 80 Baptists in suburban

Philadelphia have been seriously discussing the tremendous need for a new supportive community. They have described this community in a working paper that has become the basis for long and exciting debate. The purpose of "New Community" as presently defined is "to build and maintain a supportive community in which people of all ages, races, classes and backgrounds can live, with access to, and time for meaningful interpersonal relationships with each other," with the opportunity to develop a sound community-centered economic base.

The goals under consideration are to free members of the community from the excessive consumption cycle of society and create opportuntites to venture into creative, fulfilling work that they really want to do rather than what the corporate state and traditional life styles force them to do. Each person or family unit would own as much or as little as they felt they needed in terms of personal fulfillment and privacy. Land, buildings, automobiles, vans, tractors and other community-provided facilities would be owned by the community. Every resident would be a partner in a nonprofit corporation. Automobiles and other machines would be "rented" by the members at actual cost. It is considered wasteful and unnecessary consumerism to have each household own a car or two, or a power mower. Community members would market their skills and services in the wider community, for example: service trades, child care (for new community and larger community), low profit public food store and consultation services. Persons now considering this new life-style have expertise in several fields, for example, teaching, counseling, organic farming, arts and cultural activities for recreation and creative employment.

In regions where new communities like Columbia, Maryland, are being developed by government and private business interests, the input from church groups about the nature and *ethos* of such communities could be highly significant. Discussion about supportive communities is needed to give direction in terms of humanization and new life-styles that counter competition, consumerism and dehumanization of self and neighbor.

Women's Liberation and Women in the Churches

Tensions between the clergy and the laity are present in all denominations. A case in point is the conflict between pastors and organized church women. The Women's Liberation Movement is moving into the churches as Roman Catholic and Protestant women are becoming conscious of the fact that they have been suppressed and oppressed by church structures and doctrines. Voluminous studies are under way to document and protest the discriminatory employment practices of the churches and the lack of representation of women in the decision-making bodies of the churches. Women scholars are writing books and articles challenging existing theological-biblical interpretations of the role of women. Ecumenical commissions and denominational task forces are pressing for changes that will free women to be full members of the Body of Christ to make their unique witness, and to undertake their various ministries.

Society dictates that women are to fulfill themselves through husbands and children, the inference being that women do not become persons on their own. The church's practices and teaching reinforce this concept of womanhood, stressing woman as the servant and helpmeet of man, or as temptress as in the Genesis story. Although the usual parish program divides the membership on the basis of age and sex, the institutional church centers much of its organizational life in the traditional family which has been a major exploitive force.

Pressures have mounted within the last decade in several denominations to disband women's organizations. But the fact remains that women need their own organizations more than ever today for development of leadership and as a supportive community. Women's associations and circle groups in the churches should be aware of the goals of the various groups in the Women's Liberation Movement. Hopefully some church women will want to establish contact and rapport with them.

THEOLOGICAL REFLECTION

Can the present institutional church become a supportive community? Many would sorrowfully admit that the chances are slim. Some would look elsewhere for it —among one's professional peers, in the community of work, perhaps. Some would hold out the hope that a "saving remnant" of the church has the potential for becoming a supportive community. In our theological reflection we consider two bases for such hope—the New Testament teachings about *koinonia* (fellowship) and *diaconia* (service). These Greek words have reassurance for our age of change and shifting relationships and values.

The *koinonia,* as Paul Lehmann writes in *Christian Faith and Christian Ethics,* is a way of spelling out what "the body of Christ" means—in the concrete human situation in which it becomes possible for human beings to be open for one another and to one another. It "is a laboratory of the living word in man's interrelatedness. . . . We are what we are in and through God's action in Christ, bringing our authentic humanity to pass through authentic belonging." In Ephesians 4:16 Paul writes about this fellowship, "joined and knit together by every joint with which it is supplied (so that) when each part is working properly (it) makes bodily growth and upbuilds itself in love." In the context of loving and continuing concern for the other, koinonia members find strength to cope with life's complexities and conflicts, and bear the psychic strain of crisis. They also find help in facing the ethical decisions of daily living. In the koinonia human differences cannot disrupt or destroy the relationships; these become evidences of the reality and maturity of the fellowship.

The supportive community equips its members for the work of ministry, each being the priest of his neighbor; each discovering in community what is to be done in faithful and ethical response to what God is doing. The members are accountable to God and to each other and know that they will be held accountable by the fellowship.

The World Council of Churches has developed several documents commenting on the *diakonia* and the *diakonos* as they are used in the New Testament.[2] *Diakonia* is one of the many aspects of Christ's whole life and work, and of his reign and intercession as the Lord of all. Christ's *diakonia* is the basis for our reconciliation with our brothers and with God, the creator of all humankind. In these New Testament terms the whole life of the church is to be a *diakonia,* a compassionate and humble service to all in need, an outpouring of the body of Christ in response to the needs of the world. Christ healed the sick, fed the hungry, washed the feet of his disciples. Christ himself is the *diakonos* not only of

---

[2] *Nine Reflections on the Ministry of Deacons in the Church,* Division of Studies, World Council of Churches, September 1964. Used by permission.

the Jewish people, but of the world's needy. The *Christos* is present in the very persons of the poor and oppressed (Matthew 25:31 ff).

Protestant and Roman Catholic theologians in the Netherlands have given the world exciting new ideas about the church as the servant of the world through the ministries of the laity. J. C. Hoekendijk in *The Church Inside Out* believes that only by being the servant community can the church justify her life. "If someone asks where the church is, then we ought to be able to answer—there where the people are emptying themselves, making themselves as nothing, serving those who suffer and demonstrating with their lives their solidarity with others . . . like her Lord the church gives her life for the other, saved only where she is prepared to lose herself."

SUGGESTED APPROACHES TO CHAPTER 4

As old, familiar patterns of life change and decline, new regenerative forms are building up. The pressure of these forces will help us to break out of the old walls and reshape what can be renewed. There are signs of renewal which Christians everywhere must look for. Many new strategies for action are at hand: some are being developed by the laity working in distinctly secular groups. A few of these are briefly described below to start local groups of laity thinking in new directions about the relation of their faith to the daily decisions they make in their work. The fact that many lay people are asking ethical questions should be understood by the clergy.

Lay ministries have these characteristics:

- They are initiated by lay people, not by the clergy.
- They begin with the problems lay people face in their daily work, not with a sermon or scripture.
- The laity do the talking, and the clergy listen. The usual roles of clergy and laity are reversed because only the lay people really know what the issues are.
- The problems are ethical and concrete, not general and metaphysical.
- The resolution of the problems depends upon group action and a sense of corporate ethical responsibility.

1. Bring together small working parties of lay people who have similar or related vocations and/or community interests to talk about their work, to think together about their ministry.

Those interested in housing, for example, could include contractors, carpenters, men and women working in real estate, planning, banking. Those in the teaching field could include principals, PTA members, coaches, school board members and clerks as well as teachers. The National Council of Churches report entitled, *Listening to Lay People*[3] should be read and discussed by lay people in all denominations and in large and small churches and communities. It could be the text for these working parties. Groups of lay people could begin meeting in the homes of members to talk over the report and how it applies to the work they do. Through the National Council of Churches and a special Task Force of the General Board some local and regional assistance will be available. New models of lay ministry will be developed within the next two to three years, as groups of lay people get together to work on some strategic plans for influencing and changing the institutions and organizations to which they are related. This new ministry of the laity would be indeed a fundamental aspect of the church's renewal.

---

[3] *Listening to Lay People,* compiled by Cameron P. Hall. (New York: Friendship Press, 1971).

2. Appoint observers from local congregations to attend meetings of professional, scientific and technological societies. *Purpose*—to listen and learn about the problems, ethical issues, changes, arising in various professional groups. Most sessions of such meetings are open to visitors. Concurrent workshops can be held during such meetings to bring together the church observers with students, seminarians, ethicists and theologians. Workshops would consider what the professionals are thinking, and provide authentic encounter, which is rarely possible when professionals are invited to come to the church. Whose "turf" it is changes the content and the tone of the meeting.

Example: For a decade the United Presbyterian Church brought together lay persons and clergy to be observer-participants in the national meetings of the American Institute of Planners (AIP). As these national assemblies met in different parts of the country, many church members were made aware of the goals and problems of this professional group that is responsible for regions and communities of the future. Planners who were also active laymen in the churches helped to plan the workshops;

AIP officers made workshop presentations. The presence of growing numbers of people from the churches raising questions about community participation, equal opportunity housing, relocation, ecology, influenced the movement of the planning profession toward social planning and planners as advocates not of the powerful business community but of the people who lacked power. When AIP observed its fiftieth anniversary, church-related participation had become ecumenical. Church leaders had active roles in assisting AIP members in organizing an association of equal opportunity planners which met alongside of the fiftieth anniversary sessions to develop recommendations and other strategies to influence planning policy and practice. Similar piggy-back groups could hold meetings during annual meetings of state medical societies, bar associations, engineering societies and so on.

3. Lawyers are influential members of our society involved in every sort of contractual arrangement. They are also present in significant numbers on church rolls. Although bar associations have competent and effective committees on ethics to "police" and control the personal-professional conduct of their members, new ethical questions

concerning the large issues of social justice have required new approaches. Within the last decade, lawyers have organized work specifically on civil rights issues and the welfare rights of the poor. The Lawyers' Committee for Civil Rights under Law, organized nationally in 1963, has defended the legal rights of the poor and disadvantaged in the South, as well as the major urban areas across the country. Lawyers have taken on all kinds of problems, from school desegregation, housing discrimination and unfair employment practices, to investigation of police brutality and malconduct. The Center for Law and Education is participating in litigation across the country that challenges the present quality of public school education for disadvantaged children.

The Center for the Study of Responsive Law is another example of a new form of public advocacy. Organized in 1968 by Ralph Nader, the Center investigates deficiencies of government and corporate bureaucracies. It has already uncovered many of the frauds which victimize consumers.

Action Needed Now: Convene groups of lawyers and judges in your community to reform the penal system. Begin by investigating the demonic and dehumanizing system of corrections including: procedures in the courts, conditions of jails and prisons, treatment of released offenders, and so on. In one community a group of judges volunteered to go to jail for 24 hours to experience themselves what happens to the persons sentenced in their courts. Judges reported that the experience was shocking and terrifying. Action could be expanded by involving groups of concerned lay persons to be "court watchers," noting abuses in the system.

4. The office of deacon carries different functions and meaning in the various churches. In some they assist regularly with the worship; in several denominations deacons are assigned financial responsibility and handle general disbursements for the church as well as handling funds to assist the poor. In others they visit the sick and shut-in members.

These established roles assigned to deacons do not free the congregation as a whole from its diaconal responsibilities, or separate worship from witness and service. All members have special functions to fulfill in the body of Christ. Deacons could be sent out as scouts and messengers, to discover human needs and involve the whole laity in tackling the root causes of poverty. They can be important links with the secular world as well as the "ministers to the poor of the congregation."

Many church members currently think of deacons as "the feet and the hands" of the congregation. The redefinition that we propose includes an analytical-reflective function to inform, to develop strategy, to analyze what membership in the body of Christ really means. We submit that this goes far beyond "service" as most church members think of the term. Each Christian is called to mission and service. Each Christian is expected to seek in daily work, home, community involvement, ways of expressing love of neighbor. The diaconate has the particular responsibility to keep this concern for others before all the people of the congregation by leading and guiding them in ministry.

5. Form a "think tank" to consider: The Future of Our Community—Our Community in 2020. Planners, businessmen, builders, editors, students, politicians, have a special stake in the future. Let them pose the questions and encourage church lead-

ers to listen. More than one meeting would be required even to open the subject. The format could be a series of panels and/or working papers. The purpose would be twofold: (1) to sensitize members to need for change; (2) to humanize processes by which changes occur. Recommendations might be developed for local or regional planning commissions, particular professional groups —local medical society, local bar association, political party caucus groups. Retirees should be invited to use their accumulated experience, wisdom and skills for future direction. *Future Shock,* by Toffler, could be the text for congregational study. A church in Western Ohio had a series of discussions on this "best seller" in the monthly meetings of the church boards and in adult Bible study groups. It changed their outlook!

6. Form a task force on the role of women in society and in the church—purpose: (a) to analyze the present place of women and changes which are occurring in society and in the church; (b) to identify the ways in which churches contribute to the oppression of women or to their fulfillment; (c) to develop supportive "sisterhoods" of women for new leadership in the churches,

particularly in policy-making bodies; (d) to establish contact with secular Women's Liberation groups. There is strong evidence that many women's organizations in the churches stand in the need of change and renewal. The independent work of a task force on women could help in this renewal; it could energize plans and personnel to move the traditional church women's groups into the new age. It could make a strong appeal to young women, many of whom are interested in the Liberation Movement.

7. Start new coalition groups of concerned people. Clergy and laity from clusters of churches could meet informally to think about the kind of renewing and retooling needed in the church. They could bring together the numbers of Christian people who have both the desire and the collective capabilities to rouse the church from its complacency and its discouragement and help it to respond to the opportunities which make this age so perilous and challenging.

To summarize what we have attempted to suggest about the servant church and the supportive community:

1. There is a rhythm in the lives of Christians. We gather for worship, prayer,

confession, communion, thanksgiving, to prepare ourselves for our work in the world—engagement with "powers and principalities," complex political processes and appalling human need and sin. Our ministries in the world send us back to the sanctuary for recommitment, renewal, forgiveness—to be sent out again, and again.

2. A major role of the church is to become fully aware of what is needed to make our society human. Because of what the church knows about the gospel and the liberating love of Jesus Christ, the church should have particular knowledge and sensitivity about what is truly human, how a society becomes truly human.

3. The church must take leadership (through its members who work in the world) in defining social values and norms for responsible social planning and social policy. The church has a continuing concern about justice and the common good.

4. Criteria and guidelines for responsible social policy and social action should be defined within the Christian community.

5. The church communicates its knowledge and concern about human matters through the lay people who work in and with the structures of society. They are God's wit-

nesses. Within the supportive community knowledge is shared, public issues are faced, new criteria and strategy are devised, and the members are empowered to do what faith and justic require.

chapter ·5·

GETTING DOWN TO CASES

There are many expressions of faith and justice which could be analyzed in this concluding chapter. We have chosen two because (a) they are of national and historical importance; (b) they show how cooperative, corporate efforts can produce social change; (c) they have profound theological meaning as an example of an affluent society's empathy with the poor. The third example is a model for congregational planning for mission, found at the end of this chapter.

Justice For Agricultural Workers: Case No. 1.

California agriculture is a big business, accounting for 33 percent of the jobs in the state. Today it is more accurately described as *agribusiness,* with the interlocking interests of land owners, food processors, food marketers, banks making agricultural loans, food transporters, the pesticide industry, the farm machinery industry and universities doing agricultural research. Farms are getting larger and fewer. Labor saving machines are replacing farm workers, and as mechanization of the farm increases more and more workers are out of jobs.

Under these circumstances the small grower and the farm worker are penalized. The small grower gets a very small return for money and energy invested, and incurs high risk. Usually, the farm worker must take the wages offered him by the growers, and earns about $2,000 or less a year for hard seasonal work, with no pension plans, health benefits, job security or vacations with pay.

Most of the agricultural workers are Mexican-Americans who have followed the harvesting season with their families and lived in misery and a mounting simmering anger in the squalid housing provided by the grower.

In 1962 Cesar Chavez decided to do something about the conditions of farm workers. He left his job as an organizer for the Community Service Organization and moved with his wife and eight children to Delano, California. They lived on their meager savings, while Chavez began to build a self-supporting organization of farm workers, strong enough to bargain with employers for better wages and working conditions. The National Farm Workers' Association had its first formal meeting in September 1962 in Fresno with an attendance of 287. By August 1964 Chavez had 1,000 members, each paying $3.50 a month in dues and participating in a credit union and insurance plan. A year later there were 2,000 members and a union newspaper called *El Malcriado* (The Misfit).

In September 1965 the now famous Delano Grape Strike began. It was at first a joint effort by the Agricultural Workers Organizing Committee (AWOC) of the AFL-CIO and the independent National Farm Workers Association (NFWA). The two organizations merged into the United Farm Workers Organizing Committee of the AFL-CIO, with Cesar Chavez as director. As a result of the Delano strike and the several boycotts related to it, there were union representation elections, bargaining and contracts signed with ten wine grape growers (Gallo, Masson, Christian Brothers, Almaden and others). In the spring of 1967 the organizing efforts focused on the table grape growers. These growers are vulnerable to strikes because table grapes require careful cultivation and hand picking.

Chavez applied pressure first on the largest United States table grape producer, the Giumarra Vineyards Corporation. To get around the boycott, Giumarra started using the labels of other growers, a violation of Food and Drug Administration rules. As a counter move, Chavez supporters appealed to the stores not to buy any California table grapes. By summer of 1968, table-grape sales were down 12 percent and dropped to 15 percent by July 1969; 80 to 90 percent of the grape workers had left the fields to join the strike. Meanwhile Giumarra recruited workers from Mexico to break the strike and the struggle was on. Since farm workers are excluded from the National Labor Relations Act, the growers claimed that there was no real labor dispute. Crucial factors were the lawsuit in the summer of 1969 against the Department of Defense to stop the Pentagon from buying table grapes, and the plight of the small table-grape grower who is usually a field worker himself.

During the five weary years of the grape strike and boycott the grape issue became *La Causa,* with the many characteristics of a religious crusade, and *La Causa* became Cesar Chavez's whole life. The marches of the strikers and their sympathizers, the picketing of market chains were like religious pilgrimages, dramatizing the workers' plight and the aspirations of five million Mexican-Americans to human dignity, recognition and a living wage.

In February 1968, Chavez began a 25-day fast "as an act of penance, recalling workers to the nonviolent roots of their movement." The fast further dramatized the issue of the powerlessness of the Chicanos. When Chavez ended the fast with Holy Communion, Senator Robert Kennedy knelt beside him and 8,000 other followers joined them in Delano's Memorial Park.

A devout Christian, Chavez read widely in Roman Catholic writings, particularly the papal encyclicals. Of particular significance to his movement were *Rerum Novarum* published by Leo XIII in 1891 affirming that the rich had made slaves of the poor and that every man has a right to a living wage and human comfort, and *Quadragesimo Anno* by Pope Pius XI in 1931 restating the right to a living wage and criticizing limitless free competition due to economic despotism. Chavez was the son of migrants and his own childhood parallels the experiences of his people.

In late July 1970, farm workers and table grape growers signed an agreement in Delano, California, that both sides declared brought a new day to American agriculture. Twenty-six grape growers, representing 35 percent of the industry, signed contracts with the United Farm Workers Organizing Committe: the first successful union in the history of American agriculture.

Cesar Chavez approached the problems of the workers in depth, understanding and taking into full account the many needs of the workers and their families. He established a credit union, a cooperative store, a newspaper, health clinics, and campaigned for voter education and registration. Since the strike the union has been working to feed, house and find jobs for the members. The strike has raised wages and improved working conditions. It has focused national attention on a problem which most of us would overlook.

These efforts have inspired and energized agricultural workers in other parts of the country. Strikes and marches have occurred in Texas, Michigan, Wisconsin and Florida to challenge and change the existing system of economic exploitation, and empower the migrant workers themselves to improve and humanize their situation.

The Farm Worker Organizing Movement and Its Significance

1. Pluralism vs. Integration.

The case of the grape strike and boycott points up the long, bitter struggle for identity and self-determination by minorities in the United States. The rebirth of our society requires that middle class whites who have dominated all aspects of it perceive a common humanity and history *through* the experience of blacks, Chicanos and Indians. It is important to understand and cherish the pluralism that we once disregarded and tried to eliminate in the melting pot. In this new pluralism each group should be free to develop its own culture while making its own special contribution to the whole society. This philosophy breaks sharply with the old theory of racial integration, which really was another form of domination by whites, since it assumed that all nonwhites would be molded into established Anglo-Saxon patterns.

2. Significance to All Poor.

"Ya Basta!" (Enough already!), "Huelga!" (Strike) are more than battle cries of the United Farm Workers Organizing Committee: they signal the emerging power of people who have been empowered to take a rightful place among peers and equals. They are signs of the emergence of a people who claim the right to determine what course of action is necessary for selfhood. Although farm workers are but a small segment of the poor, UFWOC symbolizes the hopes of many disenfranchised poor. The corporate farm is also symbolic of the power which poor, powerless people confront as they attempt to achieve their "rightful share" of the earth's riches. Because farm workers have not been covered by the Labor Relations Act to provide them with a means for organization and real negotiation, it was important to support them in the boycott, their only weapon. The boycott dramatized the disparity between the seasonal workers and the multimillion-dollar agribusiness. The boycott also pointed up the necessity for federal legislation to provide farm workers with bargaining rights and other forms of protection afforded to other workers.

3. The Plight of the Small Grower.

The small grower and the farm workers have been hurt by the whole system of corporate farming and agribusiness. As agriculture becomes more and more mechanized, there is reason to believe that the small grower will be placed in the same economic squeeze as the farm workers. Both groups compete with the low cost of farm labor in foreign countries and import regulations, without the protection of national legislation. Federal farm subsidies, government aided agricultural research, all benefit the big growers and further depress the small growers. The small growers should be encouraged to organize marketing cooperatives to participate with some strength in price setting and getting a fairer return for their crops.

4. The Boycott and the Third World

The great movements for independence, self-development and freedom in the Third World cannot be separated from the struggles of the poor and powerless in the Western world. We have formed the habit of thinking and acting in response to the needs of Latin America, Africa and Southeast Asia in traditional white Western middle-class terms. Our theories and policies for "development" assume that the Western world's values, styles of life and technology are what will be good for the Third World and what the Third World wants and needs. The thousands of Americans who refused to buy and eat grapes got a sense of being part of the world-wide struggle.

5. The Significance for the Churches.

For many years denominational groups and church councils have supported "migrant ministries." Many concerned church women have volunteered many kinds of services particularly aimed at ameliorating the hardships under which migrant farm workers have lived. Some church groups have worked for protective legislation, safe, decent housing and sanitation. But such efforts in the past were small and scattered. What was done did not change the system; it helped to perpetuate the paternalism of well meaning whites. What was remarkable about the strike and the boycott was that (a) it actually empowered the people affected by the system to help themselves; (b) it focused national attention on an entrenched evil; (c) it gave everybody a chance "to do something," and (d) it brought about real social change.

Attack on the Health Empire: Case No. 2

This case material deals with a subject of great personal and national interest—health care. It probes one aspect of the health scene—the quality and availability of hospital care for the poor in Washington, D.C. It exposes the chaotic state of U.S. medicine, once the pride of our country.

In July 1969 President Nixon officially declared a "National Health Crisis." The mass media rushed to produce TV documentaries and magazine exposés of scandalous neglect, particularly of the aged ill in nursing homes. But millions of Americans from personal experience have known that health care has been in a state of crisis for at least two decades. The world's richest nation with the most advanced medical technology has no national health policy. The treatment of disease for a fee has so preoccupied the providers of health services that all but the very wealthy have become the victims of the crisis. Today health care everywhere in the United States is scarce, expensive, fragmented and available only in an atmosphere of mystery and unaccountability.

The Health Empire is the gargantuan complex of physicians and surgeons, in private practice and government service, hospitals, clinics, nurses, technicians, medical schools and research, drug manufacturing and sales, suppliers and manufacturers of hospital appliances and equipment, Blue Cross-Blue Shield, and other insurance companies selling health and accident insurance. These parts of the empire interlock. Together they constitute the largest single employer in the United States, and the second largest item in the gross national product. The fact that they operate relatively independently, on a self-regulating basis, outside of any control, makes us the consumers and patients powerless to make our needs and dissatisfactions known, without trustworthy guidance through the maze of products, practitioners and services. The victims of this non-system are not only the poor, the blacks, Puerto Ricans and Chicanos who cannot afford to buy what the health industry sells, but also the millions of middle-class and working class people.

It is estimated that every day some three million Americans go out to find some form of medical care. Only the lucky ones find it. Another twenty million Americans probably ought to get into the daily search but are too sick, too poor, too dispirited to try. For many, medical help is found only at the price of humiliation, dependence or bodily insult.

In 1968 after the 1967 exposé of conditions at New York City's Municipal Hospital, the Health Policy Advisory Center (Health-PAC) was set up to meet the demand for some ongoing analysis of the city's health policies and services. The staff of two began by issuing a monthly Health-PAC Bulletin summarizing their findings and recommendations. A number of medical, law and nursing students began working with them. The Center's research and analysis activities have grown to include many educational projects, seminars for students and community health workers, and direct technical assistance to community groups, students and hospital workers who want to change the system.

In 1970 two staffers of Health-PAC wrote a book, a major critique of health care in New York City, *The Health Empire,* by Barbara and John Ehrenreich, published by Random House. The Bulletin and the book have been widely read, and continue to make waves in medical seas. But equally significant are the coalitions that have been formed with Welfare Rights groups, and growing numbers of medical students who oppose the present oppressive system of care. While New York City's health system is unique in our country in that it has more doctors, more hospitals, more medical schools, and more people than any other city, what has happened in New York City is prophetic of what is beginning to surface in many other major cities. The experiment in Washington, D.C. is an important bit of evidence that a health movement is alive and growing fast. Health-PAC's mission is to serve and encourage this movement, and to relate it to other movements for radical social change in America. Through coalitions of concerned groups (including church bodies) the goal is the development of grass roots people's organizations to restructure American institutions.

In Washington, D.C. two grass roots Welfare Rights organizations became convinced that their members were being regularly deprived of adequate care in the district hospital. They compiled a long list of grievances against the hospital, more than enough evidence that the hospital was providing substandard, shoddy service. Three lawyers interested in advocacy law worked with the groups, helped them to document their grievances and found out when the hospital would be inspected for renewal of its accreditation by the Joint Commission on Hospital Accreditation. This agency is appointed by the American College of Physicians and Surgeons. By contract it inspects all hospitals and must approve them as complying with standards set by the American College of Physicians and Surgeons. Only accredited hospitals are eligible to receive Medicare funds; but in many instances inspection and accreditation were quite "routine matters."

The D.C. group demanded through their lawyers the right to bring their grievances to the inspection team. A hearing was held. Patients, hospital workers, interns, medical students and patients' families testified at the hearing, citing many violations of standards. To the astonishment of the hospital board which had never before been challenged, the Joint Commission on Accreditation gave accreditation for only one year, instead of the expected five-year period. Furthermore, the Joint Commission changed its rules for accreditation making mandatory, before accreditation is given, the holding of an "information hearing." The concerted efforts of grass roots people exerted real leverage on an immensely powerful regulatory body, and the people are greatly encouraged by their success. But they are not assuming that their work is done. A "watchdog" group continues to meet and report on what it sees.

In May 1971 the United Presbyterian General Assembly adopted a comprehensive report calling for a national public policy for the organization and delivery of health services. The report and recommendations were drafted by a distinguished committee of lay persons competent in health fields.

Among the recommendations were the following:

1. The complex issue of health and health care be redefined as a public issue, affecting rich and poor alike, rather than a professional problem to be solved by a few, whether in public or private capacities.
2. The organization and delivery of medical and other health services be directly accountable to the general public at all levels of policy formulation, determination, and administration.
3. Local consumer groups be empowered, under a national health policy, to define goals and obtain what they need, as well as to check

and balance the power of the providers of health care services.

4. There be systematic efforts to develop an informed public which has increasing competence to make wise decisions and to create systems conducive to personal and corporate health.

5. Quality control of services delivered be established through organized and objectively administered consumer and professional medical evaluation.

6. There be flexibility and pluralism in the policy-making organization of the system to allow for regional differences and changing definitions of consumer demands and provider services.

7. There be established national guarantees and mechanisms for assuring individual and consumer rights in the development and execution of policy.

The Presbyterian body further recommends that:

Comprehensive health care for all persons include at least these elements: aid in growth and development, nutrition, prevention of illness, periodic diagnostic evaluation, treatment of disease, extended and home nursing care, rehabilitation, long term care for chronic disorders, and the appropriate social and economic provisions to make these feasible in the life of a person and his household.

There be comprehensive, coordinated planning and administration of health care with publicly disciplined participation of practitioners, support personnel, neighborhood ambulatory care units, general hospitals, medical research and teaching centers, and other specialized, formal and folk resources, to maximize the appropriate utilization of each and to achieve functional cohesion.

There be such public investment in financing health care services that every person may be assured quality comprehensive health care, independently of an ability to pay; and, without discrimination because of economic status, color, sex, religion or political affiliation.

A national health agency be empowered to provide leadership in developing and progressively refining objectives, standards, and methods of financing health care; and to regulate the financial operations of the health care system, so that appropriate economies may be realized and accountability to the consumer communities assured.

THEOLOGICAL REFLECTION

It may be that our reading of the signs of the times will persuade us that we are living "between the times." There are strong apocalyptic aspects about this age to be studied in such books as Paulo Freire's *Pedagogy of the Oppressed,* and Richard

Harris's *Justice—The Crisis of Law, Order, and Freedom in America.* "Something Has Gone Terribly Wrong in America," the title of the Harris document when it was first published in *The New Yorker,* strongly conveys this feeling of pessimism and fear that American democratic processes do not work anymore.

Apocalyptic signs are clearly to be seen in what is happening in Latin America as well as in our own Southwest. No longer are misery and oppression quietly accepted by Indians, Chicanos, Colombians, as their lot in life, or the will of God. Their suffering becomes instead the rallying force for the creation of a new society. And those Christians—Catholic and Protestant—who stand with them, who become the sufferers, are indeed God's witnesses, the suffering servants of God who will bring forth justice to the nations and know not failure nor discouragement until they have established justice in the earth (Isaiah 42:1 and 4).

Throughout the Bible great concern is shown for the poor and oppressed. The good news proclaimed in the New Testament is specifically addressed to the poor. God chose the enslaved people of Israel not because of their merit, but because of their need. The have-not nations of the ancient world, Babylon and Assyria, were God's instruments for waking up Israel, reminding her of her faithlessness. Today our nation's poor and dispossessed, and the deprived nations of the Third World have a message for the affluent nations that cannot be disregarded.

Pope Paul's Encyclical *Populorum Progressio,* issued March 26, 1967, followed the Second Vatican Ecumenical Council. This teaching identified the church with the poor and oppressed of the world, calling for audacious transformation and a profound renewal of the church; it defended rebellion against tyranny and denounced "international monopolies and the imperialism of international finance." The encyclical affirmed the outcome of the struggle of the oppressed for justice as a new standard by which the mission of the church would be judged.

Many church members have been inspired by the life and example of Father Camilo Torres Restrepo, the revolutionary prophet-priest of Colombia, whose total identification with the oppressed became all-out commitment to action for change. After years of pastoral work and study as a sociologist Father Torres came step by step to realize that justice for the people of Colombia could only be achieved by opposing the citadels of political power. He ended his life in armed rebellion against the oppressive system, giving up his priestly functions for the way in which he believed he could best serve the people. Thoughtful churchmen pondering his ministry and servanthood have observed that such total identification with the poor may be the key to breaking out of the tragic barriers of privilege and poverty which have separated the human family for centuries. We live perilously between the times, but Christ is our hope. Christian hope empowers us to love our neighbor, stand with the poor, and survive without paranoia over the present, or despair for the future.

Cesar E. Chavez has written: "What do we want the Church to do? We don't ask for more cathedrals. We don't ask for bigger churches or fine gifts. We ask for its presence with us, beside us, as Christ among us. We ask the Church to *sacrifice with the people* for social change, for justice, and for love of brother. We don't ask for words. We ask for deeds. We don't ask for paternalism. We are for servanthood."

POSSIBLE APPROACHES TO CHAPTER 5

1. The multi-approach.

Many of the big complicated issues which the churches have tried to work on seem to create only controversy and frustration. People back away from concerns that they can't personally affect. The Grape Boycott and the Health Care Protest have given all sorts of people a chance to be identified with the poor; and to feel that even their small efforts were useful in supporting movements for social justice and effecting change.

These protests created commotion and controversy in families, churches and social gatherings. Here is a listing of some of the kinds of action taken in support of the United Farm Workers Organizing Committee. These techniques can be applied to other issues:

- Picketing at supermarkets where grapes were sold.
- Distribution of handbills about the strike at markets.
- Distribution of information kits at churches.
- Conferences with owners and managers of food chains to get them to agree to

remove table grapes from their markets.

- Regular and spot checking of food stores to see that managers kept to their agreements not to sell grapes.
- Personal pledge not to buy or eat table grapes.
- Work for national legislation for fair labor standards and collective bargaining rights for all agricultural workers through letters and personal conferences with members of congress.
- Conferences with groups of small growers urging them to form marketing cooperatives.
- Monitoring of schools, hospitals, camps, to urge boycott of grapes.
- Committees appointed to stay in contact with agricultural problems especially in pressure areas.
- Publication of appeals to stop buying and eating table grapes.
- Recruitment of speakers and liaison persons to interpret the strike and boycott.

2. The cases of the grape strike and boycott and health care protest illustrate the world-wide movement toward self-determination and control by the people.

Only as the people organized themselves

and built a cooperative base for action could their status change. Concerned white middle-class people could help but the leadership had to be taken by the poor. Few of us in the churches here or overseas have thought about what community control really means. How do the people oppressed by American corporations, the health empire, or agribusiness get liberated? How do they get and keep community control? What would a "people centered" board of directors look like? Try a new simulation game to work out various models of community control for a comprehensive Health Care Center.

3. A look at our personal values and way of life.

The social changes illustrated in the two cases suggest the need for most of us to do some serious questioning about our own personal values, the freedom to let go of cherished opinions, live through uncertainty and perhaps chaos, and come out with new commitments and new viewpoints. For example, action groups could think through the options that consumers, small farmers, small manufacturers face as they confront the giant corporation, agribusiness or the health establishment. What is the responsibility of the consumers who are also of the Christian community? Do we opt for new life styles, try new ways to earn and spend? Does progress mean more consumerism? Do "goods" make the good life?

The approach then taken by many religious sisters, lay people in Protestant and Catholic churches, ministers and priests is to fight the institutional violence and to discover cooperative, nonprofit, noncapitalistic ways of providing the services that a human society requires.

A Model for Local Church Retreats

To aid local congregations in analyzing their purpose and mission, Columbus Presbytery prepared a model for an eight-hour leadership retreat that has been extremely useful to a variety of churches. It suggests both the *content* to be covered and the *methods* to be used to set the scene for reflection and analysis. Excerpts of the Columbus Presbytery model follow:

I. *Opening Rites*—Songs and Liturgy

II. *Introductions*—Structured Conversation. The purpose of this retreat is to set objectives for the church as it engages in mission. To do this, we have to have data about ourselves and our task. This requires careful listening to each other.

1. Your name, what is your work or task in the world, and what event in the last two years do you find to be the most significant? (After about 10 people have answered these questions, get someone to recite names and events, to help them to test out their listening ability.)

2. Your name, what is your primary task in the church, and where would you point as a sign of renewal in *the church?* (*The church* meaning not only a local church but the whole church around the world.)

3. Today, what is the chief problem our local church needs to face?

4. In light of these problems, what is the chief gift (resource, strength) of our church? (If the group struggles with this for a while, hopefully they can see that the chief problem is in part the chief gift they have.)

III. *Contextual Statement*—Plan for our 8 hours together—This diagram (page 134) should be written on blackboard or scratch pad. The explanation follows on page 135.

IV. *Heritage of Local Church*—Purpose—encourage free expression by the people of their feelings, hopes, dreams, gripes, about

WHO:		WHAT IS OUR TASK:				HOW:	
Are We:	Is the church:	Art form:	Mission:	Concerns:	Objective:	When:	Who:
The people we are called to be	Role play-ing Church heri-tage	Ex. 18 13–23	What? Who? For whom?	Indivi-dual and Corporate work	Corporate struggle	Prior-ities	Roles rela-tion-ships Evalua-tion

the church. The leader explains the task of creating a story of their church—past, present and future. Then asks the group to number off from one to three, omitting task force leaders and the church's clergy.

Group #1 Story of the Church's Past (1 sentence per person)

Group #2 Story of the Church Today (1 sentence per person)

Group #3 Story of the Church of the Future (1 sentence per person)

Group #4 The task force and church's clergy serve as "enablers" to

—clarify statements by means of questions

—watch for consistency or discontinuity between groups

—ask, "How are decisions made?"

—ask, "How do you see that your description of the church is likely to be different from any other church?"

—ask, "How did past and present help you to determine the future?"

V. *Art Form* (Exodus 18:13–23)—Reading should be dramatic and lively, with participants following along with their own Bibles.

1. Who are the characters in this story?
2. What is going on in Moses' life? What is that?

3. How did Moses conceive his task? What do you think it should have been?
4. What was the model that Moses' father-in-law proposed?
5. Does this give ideas for our church?

Conclusion: This biblical story is similar to contemporary process of planning, objective setting, strategizing and so on.

1. (v.19) Envision the objectives and plan for achieving them.
2. (v.21) Divide task into manageable parts, coordinate and supervise.
3. (v.20) Establish and communicate policies and procedures.
4. (v.21) Select able men and place in charge.
5. (v.22) Delegate authority, reserving only major decisions for top administrator.
6. (v.21) Teach and show the people the work they must do.
7. Provide means for judging their performance.

VI. *Mission: What, Who and for Whom*—Structured Conversation

Introduction: Today the word "mission" is used a lot, but it would be helpful for us to think of what we mean by mission.

1. What word or two comes to your mind when you hear the word mission?

2. What activity do you see when you see mission occurring?
3. What would you say is the major task of the church?
4. If we might say that in some sense God calls us to be the church for the sake of those who are not the church, how might we minister or be Mission to them?

Conclusion: We need to keep these insights in mind as we move on toward getting out our concerns and objectives.

VII. *Concerns Workshop*—Opening Statement and Ground Rules:

All insights valuable

1. We receive all insights; we do not argue with a person over his insight.
2. Then we try to arrive at a consensus satisfactory to all.

Individual Work:

1. List your five most pressing concerns (specific problems needing attention).
2. List your own seven point program for renewing your local church, or ways of getting at the problems you cited.

Corporate Work:

List all the concerns and problems of all members, then list renewal programs until group is satisfied that all their concerns are before the group.

Get out listing of renewal programs (be sure all problems are covered in the renewal listing).

Gestalt the programmatic listing into *manageable categories* (with everyone participating, and all insights respected). Work until the group is satisfied that all real concerns are listed in meaningful and manageable categories. Priority setting comes later.

VIII. *Lunch or Dinner and Structured Conversation*—To recall and reflect on "concerns" before next session on priorities.

IX. *Objectives and the Setting of Priorities*—Rediscovery of Present Strengths, Capabilities and Resources—What we can do to reach our objectives.

Toward that end, we do the following:

1. Draw map of immediate geographical area around church building.
2. Locate our church and other churches in area.
3. Locate key points of power, key points of conflict in area (or blocks to fulfilling the mission), and key points of possibility for mission (groups and/or concerns crying for help).
4. Draw chart of church life dynamics: groups and their numbers already at work in congregation.

5. Divide into small working groups according to the categories of mission:
a. Why (state objective), b. Leaders necessary, c. Cost, if any, d. Blocks which will need to be overcome, e. Training required, f. Necessary relationship with other churches or agencies, g. Time line (indicating both starting date and completion).

Reports from each group are presented to the whole group, working with guidance of a leader who can help the whole assembly arrive at a consensus as to the priorities of mission objectives and time schedule.

X. *Evaluation of Retreat*—What was most helpful? Least helpful? What would you change?

Closing worship.

bibliography

Freire, Paulo. *Pedagogy of the Oppressed.* New York: Herder & Herder, Inc., 1970. With a foreword by Richard Shaull. One of the creative philosophers and thinkers of Brazil and Chile, now directing the Educational Division of the World Council of Churches in Geneva, Dr. Freire analyses the changes that must occur in societies as well as educational systems. "Conscientization" which is more than understanding and self-awareness is basic to human liberation and also social change.

Health Policy Advisory Committee Book. *The American Health Empire: Power, Profits, and Politics*. New York: Random House, Inc., 1970.
A devastating critique of the present "medical jungle," and the highly profitable interlocking relationships between physicians, the research and development of teaching hospitals and medical

schools, drug manufacturers, hospital suppliers, Blue Cross–Blue Shield and the large insurance companies that underwrite hospital insurance—a conspiracy that makes preventive care out of the question, and produces a health crisis for the poor as well as the middle class.

Kotz, Nick. *Let Them Eat Promises: The Politics of Hunger in America.* Garden City: Doubleday & Company, Inc., 1969. With an introduction by Senator George McGovern. The author, a distinguished Washington correspondent, tells the shocking "inside" story of hunger: how it damages the bodies and brains of its victims, how politicians and federal agency heads have battled over programs to combat it—balancing a war economy against human need. The record of public apathy and bureaucratic impotence appalls.

Reimer, Everett. *School is Dead: Alternatives in Education.* Garden City: Doubleday & Company, Inc., 1971.
A disturbing and provocative study of public education: how the schools miseducate and permanently handicap those who don't conform. The alternatives proposed depend on cooperation rather than

compulsion, and upon local rather than central leadership. Several specifics are proposed for individual action.

Townsend, Claire. *Old Age: The Last Segregation: Ralph Nader's Study Group Report on Nursing Homes.* New York: Grossman Publishers, Inc., 1971.

A stark report by one of Ralph Nader's dedicated young *raiders.* It exposes the powerlessness and hopeless isolation of the aged ill, the lack of compassion and standards for care. Correctives: public awareness and outcry and vigorous regulatory action. Specific suggestions for visiting nursing homes include what to look for, what questions to ask. A good project for young and older citizens.

. . . .

Bryan, L. Wayne. *Guide on "Faith and Justice" for Adult and Youth Groups.* New York: Friendship Press, 1972.

Corporate Information Center. *Church Investments, Technological Warfare and the Military-Industrial Complex.* New York: Friendship Press, 1972.

Hall, Cameron P. *Listening to Lay People.* New York: Friendship Press, 1971.

Halvorson, Loren E. *Grace at Point Zero.* New York: Friendship Press, 1972.

Hessel, Dieter T. *Reconciliation and Conflict: Church Controversy Over Social Involvement.* Philadelphia: The Westminster Press, 1969.

Kaiser, Ward L. and Lutz, Charles P. *You and the Nation's Priorities.* New York: Friendship Press, 1971.

Morgan, Robin, ed. *Sisterhood is Powerful: An Anthology of Writings from the Women's Liberation Movement.* New York: Random House, Inc., 1970.

Ng, David. *See It! Do It! Your Faith in Action.* New York: Friendship Press, 1972.

Patterson, J. Wilbur. *Let Faith Be Your Camera.* New York: Friendship Press, 1972.

Raines, Robert A. *The Secular Congregation.* New York: Harper & Row Publishers, Inc., 1968.

Toffler, Alvin. *Future Shock.* New York: Random House, Inc., 1970.